LOOKING AHEAD
with hope

Best wishes

Edar

Looking Ahead with hope

*Stories of humanity, wonder
and gratitude in a time of uncertainty*

EDDIE GILMORE

CEO of the Irish Chaplaincy

DARTON · LONGMAN + TODD

First published in 2021 by
Darton, Longman and Todd Ltd
1 Spencer Court
140 – 142 Wandsworth High Street
London SW18 4JJ

© 2021 Eddie Gilmore

The right of Eddie Gilmore to be identified as the Author of this work
has been asserted in accordance with the Copyright, Designs and Patents
Act 1988.

ISBN: 978-1-913657-42-0

A catalogue record for this book is available from the British Library.

Printed and bound in Great Britain by Bell & Bain, Glasgow

INTRODUCTION

The Irish Chaplaincy began in 1957 when the Irish Catholic bishops sent nine priests to England in response to the many thousands of Irish who were coming in the post-war years to find work. My own parents were among those who came. My dad arrived from Galway in 1949 and my mum came over from Newry in 1957. Those nine priests worked chiefly with those in the construction industries and in the service sector. They would walk alongside and offer comfort to people who found themselves in a foreign land, and one in which they didn't always find a warm welcome. When my dad first came to Coventry he worked on the buildings, like many of the Irish men; and my mum took up a job in the café at Coventry railway station. They were the very kind of people that the Irish Chaplaincy reached out to in those early days. It seemed very fitting that in 2017 I found myself at the Chaplaincy in its 60th anniversary year. It was a returning to my roots and there was a sense of something coming full circle.

For twenty-eight years I had been part of L'Arche, a wonderful world-wide organisation where people with and without learning disabilities live, work and share life together, and where each person is considered to be of unique and sacred value. Relationships are very much at the heart of L'Arche, with the belief that all of our encounters have the power to touch, to transform and to heal. And just as with those missionary priests in 1957 out on the construction sites or in the hotels and cafés where young Irish immigrants were working, the image of walking alongside people is one that is much used in L'Arche.

LOOKING AHEAD WITH HOPE

I have experienced a similar spirit to L'Arche at the Irish Chaplaincy. The now predominantly lay team continues today to support Irish people in Britain, including prisoners, Travellers, and seniors. As at L'Arche, we reach out to people, especially those most on the margins, seeking to be a small sign of a more just and compassionate society; and knowing that a simple act of friendliness or kindness can touch hearts and change lives.

In my interview for the Chaplaincy I had produced a phrase that would end up a few months later in bold letters on the homepage of a new website: 'looking ahead with hope'. This book is based on a series of blogs I wrote for that website over a three-year period, during which I was especially blessed by the encounters I had with a variety of characters in a variety of places. I went into prisons for the first time and shared food and music with groups of Travellers there. I was given rice wine by fellow hikers at a remote mountain temple in Korea, and had coffee and cake with a young French couple on the top of Ireland's holy mountain. I played guitar to a crowd in an Alpine cave, and to appreciative audiences in care homes. I twice had the pleasure of dancing with a nun (a different one each time), and had the privilege of singing with a ninety-two-year-old Cork woman on her deathbed. I was constantly reminded that joy, meaning, and indeed hope, can be found in some surprising places.

I was struck again and again by the truth of a Spanish expression that I learnt following one of many special moments of encounter on the Camino, the ancient pilgrimage route to Santiago de Compostela. I'd got chatting with a Spanish pilgrim whose wife, it turned out, was from Newry and who knew one of my uncles. On telling that story the following day to a local man who I'd met through taking a detour he said to me, '*El mundo es un pañuelo*', the world is a handkerchief.

Since walking on the Camino it seemed that I was having more and more of these blessed encounters and coming across the most incredible connections. Or was it rather that I was somehow a little more open and receptive to the opportunities and possibilities which may have been around me all along, but I simply hadn't noticed them? Even in lockdown these 'chance' or blessed encounters continued. One day in an otherwise deserted seaside town I got talking to a man who, it emerged, played football for Coventry City and had been in the school team with one of my sons.

I hope that the stories contained in this book might be both entertaining and inspiring to the reader. And I hope that they might lift spirits, whilst having perhaps a little bit to say about life and faith and the human condition, as seen and experienced from my particular viewpoint in the world. I wonder as well if we may come to appreciate more and more the truth in that Spanish saying, that the world really is a handkerchief - and a beautiful one at that.

1. THE PILGRIMS' WAY

One of my hopes when coming to the Irish Chaplaincy was to introduce the practice of pilgrimage.

I had always enjoyed the L'Arche pilgrimages. Each year in May or June the normal routine of life would be interrupted and people would walk together for four days. It was a highlight of the year for me, that chance to walk with people along the North Kent coastline or through the countryside. Some years we even walked along the original Pilgrims' Way, where people have passed for hundreds of years on their way to Canterbury. Indeed each day when cycling or walking to Canterbury West station to get the train to London I would go along the road that leads down to the Westgate and towards the Cathedral that King Henry ll walked along in 1174 in sackcloth and ashes and in his bare feet, as the final atonement for his part in the murder of Thomas Becket.

As with the Pilgrims' Way to Canterbury, a pilgrimage usually has a final destination, a designated 'sacred place'. And, happily, pilgrimage routes seem usually to have lovely scenery to enjoy. But perhaps pilgrimage gives us as well a chance to reflect on what might be termed our inner journey, to become a little more aware of what is within us and around us, and to be open to receiving whatever is given. Having said all of that, I don't want to 'over-spiritualise' when it comes to pilgrimage; or anything else, for that matter. In the middle ages, when those who were able to would take a few weeks to go to Canterbury on pilgrimage, it was a kind of holiday, a chance to get out of the normal routine for a while and to see some interesting places and meet some interesting people.

And I'll bet there were some great sessions at night in the pilgrim hostels!

My pilgrimage on the Camino began in April 2015. My friend James in Australia had informed me the previous year that he would be doing the whole walk to Santiago as part of a year of celebrations leading up to his 50th birthday in May 2016 and was inviting friends from different parts of his life to walk sections of the way with him. I said I would join him as long as we could do the bit over the Pyrenees that I'd seen Martin Sheen do in the film *The Way*! He agreed and we met up in St Jean Pied de Port in France and duly spent the first incredible day walking over the mountains into Spain along the 'Napoleon route' which had only just been opened up again to pilgrims following the winter closure. It was the start of a very memorable ten days of walking and talking and meeting the world. It felt like a celebration of my own life (I'd turned fifty a couple of months previously) and a celebration of life itself. And yes, like on those medieval pilgrimages to Canterbury, there were some great sessions at night!

I had to leave James and go back to work but returned the following year to walk for another ten days. Then in October 2017 I came with my wonderful wife Yim Soon to walk the final leg to Santiago de Compostela. As with the previous two stages, one of the things I enjoyed most was getting chatting with people along the way, people from all over the world, walking the Camino for a host of different reasons. I had an almost palpable sense on the Camino of the sacred and the miraculous. It's one of those places that the ancient Celts would have described as having a 'thin veil' between earth and heaven.

With my good memories of past pilgrimages with L'Arche and from the Camino, I was keen to introduce the tradition to the Irish Chaplaincy, and to find a nice route to walk in London. Our first Chaplaincy pilgrimage day began at Kenwood House, at the top of Hampstead Heath, with a cup of tea and a Camino prayer and we set off, the young and the old, the fast and the slow, on foot or by scooter (Declan's son), through the Heath and over Parliament Hill to enjoy spectacular views of the changing London skyline. After a stretch on the roads we were back into the parks: Primrose Hill, with another stunning view from the top, then Regent's Park where we stopped by the boating lake for a well-earned lunch. Thanks to public transport (some of us making more use of it than others!) we all got to Westminster Cathedral, the physical destination of our pilgrimage, in time for Mass in St Patrick's Chapel.

Walking along busy London streets wasn't quite as pleasant as walking in the parks so for the following two years we again started at Kenwood House but kept mainly within Hampstead Heath. We cross over to Golders Hill Park where we have lunch at the café, then go back into the Heath, with our customary stop at Parliament Hill to see the view. Plus, in 2019, there was Ricky Gervais being filmed on the bench at the top. You never know who you're going to see on pilgrimage! We always finish at St Dominic's Church in Haverstock Hill where we are warmly welcomed by members of the congregation with tea and cake.

I was pleased to see how much people enjoyed the pilgrimage days. The opportunity to get out of the office and do something a bit out of the ordinary with colleagues, and to meet one or two new people and see some great views. It wasn't too far from the motivation of the medieval pilgrims, and I hoped it had been firmly established as an annual Irish Chaplaincy event.

2. FIRST PRISON GIG

My ornate, round-backed Ovation guitar which was given to me by a complete stranger has served me well over the years, and the places I've been able to share it now includes prisons.

The Irish Chaplaincy has always had a particularly strong presence in HMP Wormwood Scrubs, one of the big old Victorian prisons in London. As part of Traveller History Month in June, as well as other times, the Chaplaincy organises an event in the prison for Irish Travellers. The June 2017 event was held in the beautiful and grand old chapel, which, like all of the prison chapels I have been in, has a very special atmosphere and a palpable sense of peace and prayerfulness. The event began with a competition, with cash prizes on offer for the lucky winners, and then me performing! I'd brought my Ovation in and sang a few old Irish songs to what was an appreciative and receptive audience, and I felt more relaxed than I usually do when playing to a crowd. One of the guys told me he'd worked outside as a sessions musician and said he liked my guitar and asked if he could have a go on it. I immediately and gladly handed it over and very much enjoyed both his very proficient playing, and the friendly banter that was coming from the others: 'Fair play to ye', 'Can you sing up a bit now; we can't hear you'. The great atmosphere continued during the shared meal that followed, and one of the men I got chatting to said to me, 'It's things like this that help keep my spirits up.' It was uplifting for me too. We promised to be back for another event near to Christmas, to which one character called out, 'Well I won't be here, please God, because I'm due for release in November!'

I'd been lucky to make my first ever prison visit with Breda, who goes into all of the London prisons for the Chaplaincy. I'd followed her around the wings of London's largest prison, HMP Wandsworth, as she sought out the Irish men there and was struck by how naturally she spoke to them and how warmly and appreciatively they all responded to her. Following the Wormwood Scrubs event I was touched by an observation of Breda. She remarked on how at ease I'd been with the men, how relaxed and trusting I'd been about handing my guitar over, and what an effect this would have had on the person receiving. 'That guitar was a gift,' I explained, 'and gifts are to be shared.'

3. BUEN CAMINO

My Camino journey, which had begun over two years previously, came to an unexpected but blessed moment of completion on the evening before walking the final twelve of the 500 miles from St Jean Pied de Port in the French Pyrenees to Santiago in the Northwest of Spain. A group of us were sitting around a table in a pilgrim hostel in Pedrouzo eating, drinking, chatting and laughing: three Brazilians, two Americans, our Spanish friend Ignacio, and the Anglo-Irish-Korean combo which is myself and my wife Yim Soon. A Canadian man called Claude came and joined us. He was doing the Camino by bike so didn't know any of us who were walking but he said that he had heard the chatter and the laughter and that something had drawn him towards us.

We were sharing Camino stories and then Claude suggested that we each tell of a particular highlight of our Camino journey. Ignacio, with whom we had several times shared beer and fried octopus at the end of a long day's walk and who had often picked up the bill, confided that he had been made redundant some months previously. It was the first I knew of that. He went on to say that the Camino had taught him to see what was truly important in life, like spending time with family and friends. Nancy from New York told us about the generosity of a young German woman who both went with her and translated for her at the hospital when a foot injury had threatened to end her pilgrimage on the very first day, and then gave her a pair of sandals which fitted perfectly and in which she was able to walk until she could wear her boots again. A young man from Brazil, Mathieu, was in tears as he spoke of the death of his mother four months before and his regret at being away at the time. He went on to say that on the Camino his mother had appeared to him in a dream and had said goodbye to him. Another wonderful man from Brazil, Ariel, told us to a mixture of tears and laughter how after the Camino he was going to be a better person: 'To my girlfriend, to my parents, to my cat and my dog, even to my table.'

When it came to my turn, I explained that I was on the Camino to celebrate and to give thanks: for all that had happened in my life since I began my first stage in April 2015; for our children; and for twenty-five years of marriage. And I said that a highlight was doing this third and final stage with Yim Soon. There was loud applause and cheering in the group, and yet another toast. We had each lived something profound on the Camino and it was a blessing that we had the opportunity to share together on this last evening before Santiago something of the essence of that. I bumped into Claude again in Santiago and told him that he had been the channel of some kind of sacred energy for the group. He explained again, 'I was just drawn to something and I had to come.'

My final moment of completion was in the Cathedral at Santiago, having at first felt rather disappointed by how busy and touristy the city was. During the pilgrims' Mass I looked around and spotted Claude and several others of the amazing people we had journeyed with and felt such a deep sense of gratitude. At the end of the Mass there was the swinging of the botafumeiro, the enormous incense burner that requires seven people to lift and swing from one side of the cathedral to the other. It was truly a purification, and tears streamed down my face, tears of pure joy. As I explained to those whose English was good enough to get the pun, it was the icing on the Camino cake.

4. ADVENT: A LIGHT IN THE DARKNESS

The Christmas meal at the Italian Chaplaincy is one of the highlights of the year for the Ethnic Chaplains group, of which I'm a part. At my first such do I got chatting to Andreas, the German-speaking Chaplain in London, who I'd known in the early 1990s when he spent a year at L'Arche. We were both lamenting how Advent can get overlooked in the mad frenzy of Christmas, which begins ever earlier each year, even in Church settings. Andreas expressed his surprise that the Ethnic Chaplains had, in mid-December, sung a lusty chorus of 'O Come, All Ye Faithful' (i.e. already announcing the birth of Christ) at the end of our pre-meal prayer in the church in front of the enormous and beautiful crib in the Italian church. I couldn't remember whether or not the baby was already in the manger; he is certainly there from the beginning of December in the large crib that gets erected every year outside Canterbury Cathedral. Even the three kings arrive a few weeks early in the Cathedral precincts!

I confessed to Andreas that earlier that day I had been singing Christmas carols with an elderly Irish lady that I used to visit. She had loved it, as had I. I had to admit that to try and hold Christmas back until, well, Christmas (i.e. 25 December) was to swim against the tide. And whereas in Germany there are actually more Advent hymns than Christmas ones, the sole Advent song that most people know in English is 'O Come, O Come Emmanuel'. However, I think we can still be attentive to this most evocative and meaningful of liturgical seasons, and to the universal images that are presented. At this darkest and coldest time of the year we have the image of light and dark, and as Isaiah tells us (Chapter 9): 'The people that walked in darkness has seen a great light.' And the gospel readings tell us to be prepared, like the wise virgins in Matthew 25 who had oil in their lamps, 'Because you do not know either the day or the hour.'

Going back to Isaiah we are also given hints of the feast to come: 'A banquet of rich foods, a banquet of fine wines' (Chapter 25). Some of the gospel stories speak of a great banquet, with the poor and rejected in the seats of honour, and that's one of my favourite images of the kingdom of heaven. I'm struck as well by how in the Orthodox Church Advent is kept, like Lent, as a time of fasting and penance; the fast before the feast.

Another central image of Advent is waiting in hope, and the Church teaches us that we await two comings: the arrival of God made flesh in the form of the baby Jesus; and the second coming of Christ at the end of time. I must confess that I've always felt uncomfortable with the prospect, so vividly portrayed in the scriptures, of God coming in judgement to separate the sheep from the goats. I struggle to believe that some will be condemned to eternal punishment, and I think that both sheep and goat, light and dark, are within each of us. Having said that, I think that all that we do on this earth has profound consequence even if we may not see it at the time. The Vietnamese writer, poet and monk Thich Nhat Hanh mentions the concept of 'right word, right action', whereby we need to be extremely careful of what we say and what we do because the consequences can be for good or for ill, and we may never know what good or what ill we have set in motion. And perhaps there is an echo here of that injunction in Matthew's gospel, 'Stay awake, because you do not know either the day or the hour.'

We see in our work at the Irish Chaplaincy how a simple

word or act of kindness to a prisoner or a house-bound and lonely elderly person can indeed bring a glimmer of light into somebody's life, and can have profound and far-reaching consequences of which we might never be fully aware.

And I'll try during Advent to find places of silence and stillness in which to reflect on the incredible feast of Christmas, even if that feast begins ever earlier each year.

5. UNEXPECTED GIFTS

If, following the birth of my children, three strange people had turned up at the door with shining and sweet smelling but totally impractical presents, I'm not sure what I would have thought! Yet this is what we celebrate at the feast of the Epiphany, when we mark the arrival in Bethlehem of the three kings with their gifts of gold, frankincense and myrrh. Who are these mysterious characters who followed a star and lavished such elaborate gifts on a baby born in a dirty stable to unmarried parents? And what do these unusual events tell us about God and about our own place in the nativity story?

I tend to feel rather low at the start of January, and I always find it hard to return to work after the Christmas break. Following the hype and the excitement and then the excesses of food and drink and socialising and present-giving there is a fatigue and a kind of emptiness and a sense of 'What now?' and I find myself just wanting to curl up in bed. I received a lovely email from an old friend, Maria, who was due to travel to spend Christmas with her mother but had a viral infection and stayed at home on her own. She wrote that, 'It was amazing to live Christmas almost in my own little cave ... it gave me a new appreciation of the power of stillness and silence. I can't say that I enjoyed being so sick but I can't say that it was an unhappy Christmas either! There was something sacred about the quiet.'

It's tempting to try to run away from difficulty and pain, and I believe that the travel companies do great business in January as people plan their summer weeks in the sun to 'get away from it all'. And I must admit that I entertain some fantasies during those dark and damp days of exotic, and empty, beaches! It's not easy to live with and embrace those places of sickness, loneliness, and emptiness that afflict us all at one time or another. And it's hard perhaps to see how these could be places where God might be present in some hidden and mysterious way, and where unexpected gifts might be given.

So at the cold, dark and fallow times of the year let us be gentle with ourselves; let us dare to find places of stillness and quiet in our busy, noisy world; and let us be especially tender with one another. Let us as well be open each New Year to receiving unexpected gifts in unexpected places from unexpected bearers.

I particularly like this poem by the Jesuit Patrick Purnell:

The Magi
It was the sheer inaptness of their gifts which got her,
She giggled,
and tried,
out of politeness,
to suppress it,
failed,
And burst into laughter,
The sheer incongruity,
Of gold, frankincense
And, would you believe it, myrrh
And what she wanted was nappies
But in her laughter
They knew
That this was the place
And worshipped him,
While he wet her dress.

6. CELEBRATING ST BRIGID

I attended two quite different events on 1 February 2018 to celebrate the feast day of St Brigid, who as well as being, with Patrick and Columba, one of the three patron saints of Ireland, is the patron saint of the Irish Chaplaincy.

The first event was a Mass at Sacred Heart church in Kilburn celebrated by our own Fr Gerry. He spoke in his sermon about some of the core themes in Brigid's life and work: care for the earth, peace and justice issues, gender equality, and being close to the poor. And he told of how in the fifth century Brigid founded in Kildare a double monastery, one for women the other for men, over which she ruled as abbess. Brigid was a strong but gentle woman, a good leader, and a wise spiritual guide; she seems to have encapsulated the qualities of the active and the contemplative. She spent long periods in silent contemplation from which she drew her confidence and courage; and she took her share in the manual work of the monastery: milking the cows, shepherding the sheep and brewing the ale. She practised hospitality (which for me will always be at the very heart of Irish culture), and had a special concern for the poor and marginalised. And she was attentive to the cycles of nature, with a reverence and respect for the wonder of creation. She was also a peacemaker who often intervened in inter-tribal disputes and brought healing and reconciliation. As Gerry pointed out, Brigid was not just years ahead of her time, she was centuries ahead. She continues to bring inspiration and hope and strength, and because of all the qualities mentioned above she is a fitting patron for the Irish Chaplaincy.

LOOKING AHEAD WITH HOPE

From the church I went to the Irish Embassy to an inaugural event for Lá Fhéile Bríde, St Brigid's Day, which was a 'Celebration of the Creativity of Women'. What a celebration it was - of scientists, political journalists, artists, writers, comedians, entrepreneurs, architects, designers: Irish women who have got to the top of what still can be male-dominated fields. I was especially excited to hear three songs performed by the uniquely-expressive Franco-Irish chanteuse Camille O'Sullivan. And as I stood there in the Embassy Ballroom amidst that spellbound audience of people who were there to celebrate the gifts and creativity of Irish women, and as I thought of my own mother (another truly great Irish woman), I felt incredibly blessed: to do the kind of work I do, to meet the kind of people I meet, to have the upbringing and heritage I have.

Before we left, we were addressed by Ambassador O'Neill, and President Higgins who is patron of the Irish Chaplaincy and who gave a striking phrase in his speech, that, 'Life in love is God'. And then we were treated to another song from Camille and some final words from the host, the hilarious and lovely Pauline McLynn (aka Mrs Doyle from *Fr Ted*: 'Ah, go on …').

And one final thought: St Brigid's day marked the first day of spring in the old Irish calendar. It might seem a bit premature in the cold, damp and dark days of early February to be celebrating the start of Spring. Yet, the gradually lengthening days and the appearance in my garden of snowdrops, crocuses and even early daffodils reminds me each year that, once more, light will overcome dark, and new life shall return in that never-ending cycle of creation.

And may we continue to find inspiration and hope and strength in St Brigid.

7. LENT – A JOURNEY OF LOVE

My intention was to not drink any alcohol during Lent (with my Catholic upbringing the concept of giving something up for Lent is deeply ingrained). But Ash Wednesday in 2018, by a happy coincidence, was also Valentine's Day, so I opened a bottle of special Korean '100 Year' wine to go with the meal I'd prepared for my wife Yim Soon, who is from Korea.

On the Thursday evening we had been invited by our friends Marcus and Jenny to a restaurant as a belated gift for our silver wedding anniversary, and the delicious meal was accompanied by a very pleasant bottle of Spanish red. Friday was Chinese New Year, which is a big feast in Korea, so we had a glass of wine to go with our special new year dish of rice-cake soup. And then on Saturday I'd been invited by an old friend for a walk and a pub lunch, and we had a beer while we sat out on the terrace in the glorious early-Spring sunshine. I finally managed to abstain from alcohol on Day 5 of Lent!

I reminded myself that the first miracle of Jesus was not the curing of the leper or the giving of sight to a blind person, important as these later miracles were. Rather it was turning water into wine at a wedding feast. And it wasn't just a few bottles; it was six huge containers, probably far more than would be needed. And it wasn't just any old wine; it was the very best. Such a gesture speaks to me of a generous God who gives in abundance.

The beginning of Lent that year was marked for me as well by my mother being admitted to a dementia assessment unit. She had been in hospital following a fall and it had become clear very quickly that she would be unable to return home. I had made a few trips to Coventry since Christmas to visit and was grateful that I'd been with her for what I realised would be the last weekend she would ever spend in the house where she'd lived for nearly fifty years. I also travelled up to be with her for a weekend when she was in the hospital and it was a precious time of simply sitting together. And when I went back to her house in the evening and was looking around at the multitude of family photos on display I felt profoundly thankful for this woman who has loved me so abundantly.

As I've written already, my mum came to England in 1957, the year the Irish Chaplaincy was founded, and she and my dad were part of that mass wave of emigration from Ireland in the post-war years that led to the founding of the Chaplaincy. And today mum is just the kind of person to whom our Irish Chaplaincy Seniors' Project reaches out.

The title of this Chapter was inspired by the first of Brian Draper's excellent Lenten series called 'Lent 40'. His Ash Wednesday reflection was called 'The Way of Love', and he wrote: 'So here we are, then! Embarking together on a journey from Ash Wednesday through to Easter ... which happens also to be from Valentine's to April Fools' Day! And perhaps that's fitting. For this is a journey of love, ultimately, with an ending so seemingly foolish that, quite poetically, it's almost beyond belief.'

I like that the word Lent comes from an old Anglo-Saxon word meaning to lengthen. That is precisely what happens at this time of year; after the long and hard winter the days finally become longer and lighter. And the spring flowers are a welcome reminder that new life will surely return once more.

And whether or not we manage to keep our Lenten resolutions, may we be open in that holy season to both giving and receiving love in abundance.

8. THE BEAST FROM THE EAST

The so-called 'Beast from the East' brought to the UK and Ireland in March 2018 sub-zero temperatures, travel chaos and … the wonderful gift of snow. When I looked out of my bedroom window one morning it was to behold a world transformed. Everything looked different. There is a purity, a beauty, and something truly magical about snow. There is a particular sound as well: a sort of reverential hush. A snowfall also forces us to slow down, or to stop altogether, which may be no bad thing in a world where we seem to be in such a hurry such a lot of the time.

The freezing weather is no comfort to the increasing numbers of people sleeping rough in our cities, but for those of us lucky enough to have heated homes it is lovely to be able to curl up in the evening with a hot drink. And one of my great pleasures in winter is to sit and gaze at the flickering flames of a real fire. I was on my way to bed on the evening when the snow first fell. I knew I had to seize the moment, for Canterbury often misses out on the snow, so I got dressed again and trudged out towards the now-white slopes leading up to Kent University, which sits on a hill overlooking the town and the Cathedral. It was lovely to hear the excited shouts of groups of students throwing snowballs at each other.

Snow seems to bring out the child in us: a playfulness and a joyful and exuberant energy that can be channelled into making snowmen or sledging down the nearest hill. I bumped into friends who were dragging their little boy along on a sledge. 'I love sledging,' he called out to me. 'Oh, so do I,' I replied. Our three sledges were stored at the back of the shed now that our own children had left home. How I used to love going with them, in the winters when we were blessed with snow, to a huge 'crater' nearby and seeing how many people we could squeeze onto one sledge and then all of us crashing in a heap at the bottom of the hill. In the absence of sledging I was running down ungritted side roads near my house and seeing how far I could slide, and for a few seconds I imagined that I might be in the Winter Olympics! Who knows, we might in twenty years' time have 'freestyle street skidding' alongside curling and the half-pipe!

The rail companies were doing their best to cope, but on the train back from London one afternoon the guard announced rather ominously, 'East Kent is currently a no-go zone, and for those passengers wishing to go to Canterbury it is impossible to get there by train or bus. I advise you to get off at Ashford and wait for further announcements.' It's eighteen miles from Ashford to Canterbury and I had my fold-up commuter bike and I thought, 'Why not, it's an adventure!' An adventure it certainly was on country lanes thick with snow, and on one especially icy bend the wheels went from under me and I, and the bike, skidded several yards down the road. I got up, unhurt, and looked around at the snow-covered hills and breathed in the fresh, icy air and thought, 'What fun!' I so often battle and rage against my immediate circumstance, be it extreme weather or a tricky personal situation, and wish it was different. For once I had resolved to accept the reality I found myself in, to go with it, and to actually enjoy it.

I made it home (with, by then, very cold feet!), and I gave thanks for my heated home, and I gave thanks for the snow. And I reflected that, as in so many situations we find ourselves in, if we can manage to befriend the beast, rather than battle against it, what simple yet profound treasure lies in store.

9. ST PATRICK'S WEEK
IN PRISONS
(AND OTHER PLACES)

Our special event at Wormwood Scrubs was my third prison visit in a very busy St Patrick's Week.

Earlier in the week I'd been in a women's prison for the first time. That day had begun with our Irish Chaplaincy 'St Patrick's Coffee and Cake' morning at the London Irish Centre, which included delicious cake, a fantastic display of our work, and live Irish music – by me! From there I dashed off to catch the train to HMP Bronzefield in Surrey.

Agnes, one of our wonderful volunteers, and Karen, the, equally wonderful, RC Chaplain, had kindly invited me to join a group of Irish women for a meeting. Karen had provided tea and cake and there was a lively discussion in the room which turned at one point into a full-blown shouting match. Somehow things calmed down again and there was a chance to chat one to one with the women and to hear a bit of their stories. Some of the women there are utterly broken by what life has thrown at them. Some have children outside; and one has a pimp outside, who's waiting for her when she gets out. Some, probably most, have been on the receiving end of a lot of abuse, usually at the hands of men. I was struck by how appreciative they all were that people had come to visit them, to share a drink and a cake and a bit of time together, and to be given rosary beads and Traveller magazines. And for many of those women, they

27

will receive no other outside visitors apart from the Irish Chaplaincy.

A couple of days later I left home at the crack of dawn to arrive early at a prison in the south east of London where we had a meeting to discuss the possibility of the Irish Chaplaincy providing resettlement support for Travellers. From there it was a long trek over to West London to Wormwood Scrubs for another meeting with some prison staff, before joining our St Patrick's celebration. The event was held again in the magnificent chapel, and there was a good turnout: more than thirty men from the wings, plus various prison staff and those of us from the Irish Chaplaincy; and guests we had invited, which included somebody from the Irish Embassy and other people involved in prison work. We were treated to Irish music from Neil, Zoe and Whiskey Mick - who, it turned out, knows Shane MacGowan of The Pogues. There was Irish dancing from Grainne, one of our volunteers; then a shared meal: for me, always a crucial part of the event. The kitchen had prepared bacon, cabbage and potatoes and even though some of the guys were moaning that they had turned it into a stew it was really tasty. Breda and Liz had brought along soda bread and other nice things and it was a real feast. And Ellena went around giving out St Patrick's prayers and also puzzles, which a lot of the men enjoy doing.

There were not only Irish prisoners present. When I heard the strong Polish accent of one man I said to him, 'You don't sound very Irish but you're very welcome.' He beat his chest and solemnly announced, 'I feel Irish in my heart!' During the meal I chatted with two Albanian Gypsies (who assured me they also felt very close to the Irish!). They were the friendliest, most courteous people you could meet. I don't know what they've done to end up in prison: I don't ask; I don't need to know. For those couple of hours, we are fellow human beings, enjoying together some music, dancing, and bacon and cabbage stew. And we don't discriminate at the Irish Chaplaincy. If a prisoner registers as Irish or Irish Traveller we will offer a visit and assistance, also to their family in many cases, whatever crime they have committed. And, as said already, we may be their only outside visitor.

From the prison it was off to the Irish Embassy for the St Patrick's reception. The Guinness at the Embassy is the best I have tasted outside of Ireland so my Lenten alcohol fast was broken yet again: but actually Irish people are allowed to break it for St Patrick's Day so technically I was okay! I met a lot of lovely people, both Embassy staff and people from other Irish community organisations, and it was a privilege to be there.

The following morning I felt completely shattered and a bit dispirited, for reasons I couldn't exactly put my finger on, and I had a lot of office work to catch up with, plus another big event: the visit of nine members of the L'Arche Kent Book Club from Canterbury for lunch. Downstairs at the Irish Centre I bumped into Nora. She directs, among other things, the Irish Elders' Choir and she'd very kindly organised some of the performers at a concert we'd put on the previous summer; and it was her sister Molly who had mobilised the musicians who had played at Wormwood Scrubs. I spoke about another concert we were planning and Nora agreed immediately to be part of it again, and we chatted as well about Whiskey Mick & Co. There was something about that encounter that really lifted my spirits. The group from L'Arche duly arrived and they were pleased to see me and I was pleased to see them. I had known one of those who came, Henri, since 1988, the year I arrived at L'Arche. Such relationships run deep. Liz and Ellena had prepared a sumptuous lunch up at the Chaplaincy and it was for me a special coming together of different worlds. Gifts were exchanged. There was L'Arche beer (to be saved till Easter?!), candles and scented pin cushions for the Chaplaincy; and Irish Chaplaincy mugs and bookmarks for the L'Arche contingent. Then I took the group to John Dunne's latest 'Irish Theatre' production in the Kennedy Hall, followed by a drink in the Centre before farewells and promises to do it again soon.

The finale of St Patrick's Week was Sunday mass in the McNamara Hall at the Irish Centre celebrated by our own Fr Gerry, and attended by Ambassador Adrian O'Neill; together with an Irish government minister and the Mayor of Camden. Gerry spoke in his sermon of the work of the Irish Chaplaincy in supporting some of those Irish people in Britain who are most vulnerable and socially-excluded, and who in many cases are living lives of quiet despair; and of how we always treat people as individuals, and never as mere statistics. Mass was followed by a full Irish breakfast, laid on by the Council of Irish County Associations, which fortified us well for a St Patrick's Day parade in sub-zero temperatures due to a 'mini Beast from the East'.

Shared food and fellowship with a variety of interesting people: what better way to celebrate St Patrick's Week.

10. ST CUTHMAN'S

I've always enjoyed going to nice places for times of retreat and there was a particularly special retreat house in Sussex called St Cuthman's. On what was to be my last visit there, I had a large room overlooking the lake, around which ducks would be swooping and skimming; and I could see in the distance, through the tall trees, the hills of the South Downs.

My first task on arrival was to call my mum to see how she was getting on in her new care home, but then I switched the phone off and it remained switched off for the forty-eight hours I was there. Like many people I am often during a typical day having a quick peep to see if there are any new messages, and feeling sometimes relief, sometimes disappointment if there are not! I also resisted the urge to avail myself of the recently introduced free Wi-Fi. I did not intend to have any communication with the 'outside world', and when I awoke the following morning not knowing what time it was, I decided not to look; rather to get dressed and go outside for a walk, which is what I like doing every morning. I took the chance there, as I usually do on retreat, to slow down a bit, to look carefully and consciously, and to rejoice in the beauty of the massed ranks of daffodils in the garden and the new buds emerging on trees and bushes. I attempted to walk and to eat a little more mindfully. And I spent a bit of time just sitting in the comfortable armchair in my room, gazing out at the lake, listening to the birds. I gave thanks.

I had discovered St Cuthman's years before when I was there for a L'Arche meeting. It was a popular venue: a lovely old house with log fires in the winter, and nice food, plus tea and cake in the garden room at 4 o'clock. And there was a delightful, high-ceilinged and spacious library with huge settees, from which to gaze out at the large garden and grounds. Most of all there was a palpable sense of peace and tranquillity. The house was at one time owned by a missionary order called St Julian's and it is where people would return, exhausted, from long missions abroad in need of rest and healing. We held our L'Arche meetings in many places and they could be fraught affairs, but when we came to St Cuthman's we always seemed to have a good and harmonious gathering. I decided after that first visit that, even if it was a bit pricey, I would go there each year for a little retreat. In April 2018 I was ready, as ever, for a couple of days of solitude and rest. The previous few months had been busy at work and there had been a lot going on as well on a personal level, with my mum on that bewildering journey into dementia. A few weeks before when I'd been feeling especially weary I booked in for my two days there and that helped keep me going. When I used to give induction to the new assistants at L'Arche I always impressed on them the essential need to take care of oneself. I often have to remember to take my own advice.

I'd been at St Cuthman's in November 2016 for what turned out to be my last L'Arche meeting. A few days earlier I had seen an advert for an interesting sounding job: 'CEO - Irish Chaplaincy'. I stayed on after the meeting for an extra day and it was there that I wrote my application. I almost didn't apply, thinking that with my complete lack of prison experience I would have no chance of getting the position. I was encouraged by someone at L'Arche to go ahead with the application. I am profoundly grateful that I did, and that the application was successful.

I'm sure that we must all be affected, in body and spirit, by the physical environment we find ourselves in; so too by the history of a place. I know how much I need for my own well-being to find places where there is space, and peace and quiet, and beauty. Many of those we support at the Irish Chaplaincy are not so fortunate. One of the things that struck me most on my first prison visit was how tiny the cells were (and most are shared with another person). Prisons are also very noisy. And if I ever found myself in a room, any room, that was locked from the outside I think it would send me into utter panic. To not be able to go out for my early morning walk is utterly unthinkable. And many of those we see are 'banged up' (i.e. locked in) for up to twenty-three hours a day. Also, some of the elderly Irish we visit in London are living in material poverty. I don't know how they ended up like that. Probably it was a gradual process, a slipping through the support net of what may once have been provided by family or the wider community. We do what we can now to offer some comfort and companionship, and to try to reconnect people to an outside world which must look very alien and uncaring to them.

It was my final visit to that sacred place because it was closed soon after due to the huge financial cost of running such a big old house. I'm fortunate that I have other places where I can find my space and my peace and quiet, my places of rest and healing. But I miss St Cuthman's.

11. LETTING GO ... MOVING ON

I was sitting in my old bedroom in my childhood home for the very last time and feeling a queer mix of emotions. The room was almost bare, following the big clear out the day before. I'd had my early morning walk, along roads in Coventry filled with fifty years' worth of memories, and I'd shed a few tears as I realised it was the last time I'd be making such a walk.

We'd moved there when I was three and it was my mum's home until earlier that year. She'd spent the previous twenty years on her own in the house following the death of my dad. She'd moved into a care home and seemed to have accepted that it was the best place for her to be at that time. Or maybe she was in denial, who knows. The house needed to be rented out, so as to make the care home fees go a little further, so Yim Soon and I were helping my sister and brother-in-law with the fifty years' worth of accumulated 'stuff'. Mum kept a lot of things so there was a lot to sort through. Old school reports emerged in between thirty-year-old insurance documents. There was a copy of an Irish census record from 1911 with details of some of the Newry McStays, mum's family. And an absolute gem turned up in one envelope containing copies of birth certificates and the like. It was a letter from the British Railway Board dated September 1957 offering mum a job in the Coventry railway station café and free rail passage from Belfast. This was especially poignant for me because it was in about September 1957 that the founding members of the Irish Chaplaincy were starting to reach out to the newly-arrived

Irish in Britain. It was because of people like my mum, and my dad, coming to start a new life in a foreign land, that the Irish Chaplaincy began.

I gave thanks for my mum and dad, for all of my family and ancestors, and for the life that had been lived in that house over those fifty years. And I took heart in a comment made to me some years before by Thérèse Vanier, sister of Jean, the founder of L'Arche, when I was explaining to her the need to close Little Ewell, the big old house near Canterbury where L'Arche was started in the UK by Therese and others in 1974. 'It will be sad,' she had said, 'but that's all right; sadness is part of life.'

Acknowledging sadness and loss; giving thanks; letting go … and moving on: it is all part of the rich tapestry of our life.

12. SOWING THE SEEDS ...

People think I'm crazy when I tell them but I love cycling in London. I used to ride from home each morning down to Canterbury West station on my fold-up bike, and when I got out at St Pancras International I would cycle up through the wonderful new, water feature-filled, Granary Square development, then along the canal which would take me out close to the Irish Centre in Camden where we have our offices.

When I was out for appointments I would always go by bike if possible, whatever the weather. I must admit it's a bit more pleasant when it's warm and dry, and it's a particular pleasure in the springtime with the profusion of bright colours to be seen in gardens and parks: the cherry blossoms, the azaleas and rhododendrons, and one sight that thrills me each year and which seems especially common in the big city with its tall houses: the wisteria. Besides the beauty of the flowers and the subtle fragrance, I'm staggered by the sheer height that some of these climbers can reach. Some of them cover entire five-storey houses. I imagine it must take decades, and a lot of proper care, for these plants to get so high and to produce so many flowers. And I've read that some varieties can take up to twenty years just to produce their first flower. It struck me that the person who planted the initial seed may well never have lived to see the wisteria in all of its mature glory, or even to see the first flower. And perhaps there's a bit of a metaphor there for our day to day lives. The words we speak and the things we do might have long-term consequences, for good or for ill, that we will never live to see. A small act of kindness, a friendly word, a simple smile: these can touch, and even in some situations save, a life in ways we may never be aware of.

I'm reminded often of the words that are commonly attributed to Archbishop Oscar Romero:

That is what we are about.
We plant a seed that will one day grow.
We water seeds already planted,
knowing that they hold future promise.
We lay foundations
that will need further development.
We provide yeast that produces effects
far beyond our capabilities.
We cannot do everything,
and there is a sense of liberation
in realising that.
This enables us to do something,
and to do it very well.

The first seeds of the Irish Chaplaincy were sown in 1957 and I'm pleased to say that the plant which grew from those seeds seems to be still producing good fruit over six decades later through the tender care of some of those Irish people who find themselves most on the margins of British society. And I'm happy to have the chance now to do my own little bit to tend the plant, to water the seeds, and perhaps to sow one or two new seeds that maybe someone in the future will tend.

I'm also grateful to those people who decades ago planted outside their London houses a tiny wisteria plant which today bring me such pleasure as I cycle past in early May.

13. EAT A LOT OF RICE PLEASE!

I was told many times at the beginning of meals in Korea, 'Eat a lot of rice please,' i.e. please eat a lot. I had spent a year in Seoul with the family from 1999-2000 but had not been back until Yim Soon and I had a special two weeks together in her homeland in May 2018. It took a while after that trip for my stomach to recover from the wealth of interesting and spicy food that was given to me, not to mention the variety of alcoholic beverages that it would have been impolite to refuse! A particular Korean delicacy is raw fish and everyone, it seemed, wanted me to try it. Some of the raw fish might already be dead when it arrives on the table; some of it might be still wriggling and squirming on the plate, like the octopus legs that were put in front of me in one restaurant. 'You just need to chew it to kill it,' I was told! With raw fish the usual routine is to dip it into chilli sauce with your chopsticks; place on a lettuce leaf together with a slice of garlic, a piece of chilli pepper and a blob of rice; take a swig of soju (Korean style schnapps); then wrap up and put the whole thing in your mouth and chew away.

Some of the meals we had with others were simpler but no less generous. On top of a mountain peak an elderly man shared his flask of coffee with us and we shared our rice cakes with him. On another peak at a Buddhist temple we were given an entire meal as it was Buddha's birthday, a feast similar to Christmas. And a group of fellow hikers shared their rice wine with me. I'd discovered rice wine on my first visit to the country in 1992 when Yim Soon and I had spent a few days walking in the mountains in one of the national parks and staying in a Buddhist temple. We'd met, amongst others, a company president who was taking a month off work to walk. At the end of the day he invited us and a few other hikers to join him at a restaurant for spring onion pancakes and large bowls of rice wine. Whenever I drink rice wine now, I think of walking in the mountains in Korea.

Showing hospitality to the guest by way of offering food and drink is central to Korean culture, as it is to Irish culture; and it was interesting to see Leo Varadkar tweeting after a meeting with the South Korean Prime Minister that took place just after our trip that, 'Korea is the Ireland of Asia.' I could no more have refused my kind Korean hosts what was put before me, however much it might have been wriggling, than I could my Irish mother when offering food. Saying no would be pointless: she would give it anyway! And Yim Soon does exactly the same! And as someone who likes his food one of my fondest memories of childhood holidays in Ireland is coming to the end of a day in which we'd all been amply fed and then somehow managing to find space for the large plate of soda bread that appeared, accompanied by those immortal words, 'Ah, go on.'

Hospitality is clearly central at the Irish Chaplaincy. In our offices there was always somebody offering a cup of tea and sometimes people would bring round little treats like Danish pastries. I was touched when I first started at the Chaplaincy, and still am, by these simple acts of kindness. Food and drink play an important role too in our outreach work with socially excluded or lonely Irish people, whether that's having a cup of tea and a bit of cake with an elderly person living alone, or sharing a bacon and cabbage meal at a Traveller event in a prison.

I'm always struck by how many references there are in the bible to eating and drinking. There is the story of Abraham giving hospitality to three strangers who were actually angels in disguise: the moral of the story being that we never know when we might be entertaining angels without realising it. And Jesus seems to have been constantly sharing food with people, and oftentimes it was those people who found themselves on the margins of society with whom others refused to eat and drink.

My final family meal on that holiday in Korea was a true feast; as if all the others hadn't been! Yim Soon's eldest sister and her husband had got up early in the morning to visit the fish market, and on the meal-table later there were not just one or two but three types of raw fish. One of them was a King Crab. I think it was dead: it wasn't moving at any rate. It was actually very succulent and tasty, the legs especially. You have to work a bit with the chopsticks to get the best meat out but it's worth the effort. We ate, we drank, we shared some memories of our wonderful two weeks with these good and very hospitable people. It was with some sadness that we said our goodbyes, but how our bodies and our hearts had been enriched and nourished.

14. BELLS AND SMELLS

Buddhist temples might seem at first sight to be far removed from Catholic churches but closer inspection reveals a surprising number of similarities.

I've always loved visiting the Korean temples. They're usually found on wooded hillsides or even remote mountain tops, and they are a feast for the senses. If the food in Korea does incredible things for the taste buds, then my visits to temples are a banquet for the eyes, the ears and the nose. The bright, vivid colours in which the exterior wood is painted are especially striking, yet they give a calming effect, as do the gently sloping rooftops. You take off your shoes at the door, as indeed you do when going into any Korean dwelling, and you enter a darkened space with a lush polished wooden floor. As someone brought up in the Roman Catholic faith I am immediately at home with the massed ranks of candles; and also in common with Catholicism, in order to light a candle you are invited to make a little donation! Then there are the statues, always a central one of the Buddha, and sometimes a smaller Buddha on each side. They show the Buddha in various guises, and the most impressive I saw was on the way up a mountain. Yim Soon and I almost missed it. We had been into lots of temples by that point and there didn't appear to be anything special about this one at the side of the trail. A monk appeared and, perhaps because I was a foreigner, suggested that we go through a certain door into one of the buildings. We did as instructed and found ourselves in the middle of the temple an enormous Buddha carved out of the cliff-face of the mountain.

On approaching a temple you will often hear the sound of chanting, another similarity with traditional Catholic liturgy, and there will be the smell of incense sticks burning. And each temple has its bell, which will be rung at certain times of the day.

At one temple we were invited by one of the sisters (again possibly because of me being a foreigner) to come into the reception area for a coffee and a chat. The sister then gave us the pieces to make prayer beads. They're very much like rosary beads, except that instead of the cross there is the name of the temple where the beads were made. She also gave us each a Korean-style dish cloth that had been made at the temple and was in the shape of a little dress! One of those had pride of place at our kitchen sink for many months afterwards. Finally the sister showed us how to bow properly. In the same way that the standing, sitting, and kneeling during the Catholic mass was supposed, I think, to be a way of using the whole body during the liturgy (and not just the head: after all, the Christian faith celebrates a God that was made flesh), so the Buddhist liturgy has lots of bowing. You have to be in pretty good shape physically to bow properly. Starting from standing and bringing the hands together you crouch right down so that your head touches the floor, do certain things with your hands and feet and then stand up again. Yim Soon and I got into the routine of doing that three times in the temples we went into. Some people do a series of three thousand 'chols' (bows) which last the whole night! (All-night vigil: very Catholic!) When we lived in Korea I found a temple that was full one day of women, when there would normally only be one or two people there, and they were all doing the chol over and over again. It turned out that it was the day the high school students were doing their university entrance exam. Their mothers were doing a certain amount of chols and praying for success for their offspring (and making a little 'offering' to the temple besides). Again, nothing too

42

different from what my mum always did: plenty of novenas to St Anthony - without the bowing, mind!

Just as I like to find beauty in a church, so too I relish the beauty of the temples, and I'm reminded that it's so important for us to find beauty in our lives. Dostoevsky went so far as to say that 'Beauty will save the world.' There has always been debate and controversy in the Church about spending money on 'externals', like decoration and ornamentation. I remember as a child our priest inviting the congregation to donate money to an appeal to have some stained-glass windows put in the church. He said, 'Make the church as nice as you want your own home to be.' He got the money; the beautiful, coloured windows were installed, and they continue to being me pleasure whenever I go into that church.

One of my favourite holy places is the chapel at Wormwood Scrubs prison. You go through a series of locked gates in tall steel fences topped with barbed wire and then suddenly find yourself in a large and lofty chapel, at one end of which is a truly beautiful sanctuary in a kind of Eastern Orthodox style with icons around the walls. It's where we hold many of our Traveller events at the prison, and it's a special place in which to share music, food and companionship.

Whether it's on a remote mountain-side in Korea or in the middle of a London prison, beauty and sanctity can be found in surprising places.

15. CLIMB EVERY MOUNTAIN

'It's true; Irish people are everywhere!'

So said to me Quitterie, a Frenchwoman, who has an Irish mother, as we made our way out of Mass at La Grande Chartreuse in the Southeast of France. Quitterie is named after a popular saint in the Southwest of France where she grew up, and she has a brother named after that most famous of Irish saints, Patrick. I had just explained to her that the Carthusian monk of thirty years who had said the Mass in that incredible monastery nestling in the Alps had been born in Dublin.

We were in the Alps as part of the team organising a retreat for sixty young assistants of L'Arche. Another member of the team was an old friend of mine, Pat Corcoran, who left Cork as an eighteen-year-old to join L'Arche in France. He and I first met in 1989 when we were ourselves on a week-long silent retreat in London for new L'Arche assistants. We had chatted on the final evening and Pat had invited me to visit him in L'Arche in Paris, where he was living at the time. I duly spent a couple of days there at the end of that year as the start-point of a bit of travelling in Europe, but Pat and I lost touch. I was invited to join the Alps team for the first time in 2011, to help with the music with Peter Brabazon, a member of L'Arche in Ireland and a talented musician, and who had also been on that silent retreat in 1989. Peter and I had shared a room and had not uttered a single word to one another (we'd both taken the silence very seriously!) but had made some good music together, also on subsequent L'Arche events that we'd been on.

I had arrived at the train station at Grenoble, and caught the bus that winds its way up into the mountains to the village of St Pierre de Chartreuse, 900m above sea level, and a ski resort in the winter. As I got off the bus in the village square, Pat was there waiting to greet people, neither of us having known that the other was going to be there. He called out, 'Eddie!', and I called out, 'Pat!' and we embraced.

It was special for us to meet up again, and to do so every June, in such a beautiful place where we walk in the mountains each day with a delightful, and very international, group of people. We hike in small groups within the overall group of seventy-five and we stay in a large house in the village run by a very welcoming group from the Focolare movement. Looking out of the windows in the morning at the mountains rising up in each direction is a sight that never fails to excite me.

It's a full day on the retreat. There is (optional) meditation at 7 a.m., followed by breakfast at 7.30, and after the evening session there is a team meeting at 10 p.m. That's a kind of a French thing! It helps that they bring nice wine and cheese to it. And then there might be a bit of a sing song as well, and over the years we have had some truly mighty sessions.

There's a different speaker each year who gives a talk in the morning to the group. In 2018 the talks were given by Cariosa Kilkommen of L'Arche in France. How does this woman from the West of Canada come to have a name like that? Yes, of course, her dad is Irish! And the name means 'church of St Comán'. At 10 a.m. we assemble in the courtyard and after warm-up exercises from some energetic young Germans or French we head off on the trail for the day. On Monday it's an 'easy' walk, to test that everyone is capable of Tuesday's hike, which goes up a nearby mountain, 'La Scia', whose summit is just under 2000m. Wednesday's walk takes us to a large cave atop a waterfall, the final section of which is vertical and up a rope; and with a twenty-five metre drop if you don't do it properly. Health & Safety has clearly not made it to France! On Thursday we walk to La Grande Chartreuse and spend a couple of hours in silence in a field above the monastery, whose monks live their lives in almost complete silence (they're allowed to talk on Sundays!), and in prayer for the world, and who have been doing so for over 900 years. It's the highlight of the week for some. Friday's walk takes us around the other side of the valley, from which we can see La Grande Chartreuse in the distance, and up to a scenic point with spectacular views.

After the day's walking we arrive back at the house at 4 or 5 o'clock with that good kind of fatigue that comes from physical exertion, and then a sizeable group go for a dip in a mountain river which is absolutely freezing and absolutely wonderful. And then we return to the village to either go to Mass or to sit outside a bar in the square for a beer. 'All things in balance,' as Pat would often remind me!

Music is an essential part of the week, and I have the great pleasure to be able to lead that now together with a Frenchman, Emmanuel. Peter was 'retired' from the team, sadly, as we needed more French songs for the largely French-speaking group. Emmanuel and I make our way through the book of mainly French and English songs, plus one or two in other languages, and over the years we've added some secular numbers to the predominantly religious repertoire. I've also sneaked a few of my own songs into the book! A favourite every year is the great Proclaimers singalong '500 Miles', which I now play, amongst other places, in the Wednesday cave, some people having taken it in turns to carry a guitar up the mountain. It's one of many unforgettable moments in the week. A lot of those jumping up and down and singing along possibly don't even know what a mile is but they're quite prepared to walk 500 of them, and 500 more!

The 'Walking retreat', as it's called, is for me an experience that's similar in some ways to being on the Camino. You set off each day with a rucksack on your back, you walk in beautiful places, you encounter people along the way and share your stories with one another in a particularly intimate way; and although you may never see them again, they touch and enrich your heart.

Like the Camino, the Walking retreat is a particular time of being open to whatever gifts are given and to being surrounded by goodness. After the 2018 week I remained in France an extra day to stay with Pat and his family. He had to call in on the way back to L'Arche in Grenoble where he is the Director. A lovely young German man called Ferdinand who had been on the retreat asked me if I would give a little concert in one of the houses there. They were even able to provide me with an amp for my guitar: a guitar which, I explained to those assembled, had been given to me by a complete stranger after I'd had my own guitar stolen. It was a pleasure for me to do that, and a fitting end to the week, for our gifts are to be shared. And then I enjoyed the warm hospitality of Pat's wife Marie-Helene (like Yim Soon and me, they met at L'Arche) and their children; and I took the opportunity to have not just one but two sessions in the swimming pool that Pat had been given recently. What a gift that was!

Pat has also now, sadly, been 'retired' from the team. But whether it's with Irish people, or Germans or French, I aim to keep on climbing those mountains and singing those songs and soaking up that Alpine goodness for as long as I can.

16. WHERE'S THE BISHOP?

Mamie, who was born in Limerick in 1931 and grew up in Dublin, and is one of those supported by the Irish Chaplaincy Seniors' Project, had been convinced there was a bishop coming to visit her, and as each of the guests came into her flat and turned out not to be a bishop, she seemed to grow more and more disappointed. First in were Paul the Seniors Manager and Joe, one of our wonderful volunteers. They were followed by two special visitors from Ireland: Alan Brogan, former Dublin Gaelic footballer, and Harry Casey who works closely with the Irish Catholic Bishops' Conference; which is where she must have got the notion that there was a bishop flying over to see her. As I trooped in last, Mamie asked me, almost in desperation, 'Are *you* the bishop?'

It was part of a hugely enjoyable day spent in London introducing Alan and Harry to some of the elderly Irish supported by the Seniors' Project, in anticipation of a sponsored walk which was to take place in October 2018 to raise funds for the project and for which Alan had kindly agreed to be ambassador. Mamie proudly took us into her little back garden which had been transformed by Joe's hard work at weekends. As the illustrious party settled down for tea and sandwiches prepared by Joe, Mamie mentioned once more that she really had been expecting a bishop. Alan may be a three-time All-Ireland title holder (and he was incredibly attentive with each of the people we visited), but what Mamie wanted was a bishop!

Mamie began to tell us a bit of her story, how she and her beloved Nicholas had left Ireland in the 1960s on their wedding day to come to a new life in London. It was following the death of Nicholas in 2010 that Mamie had been supported particularly closely by the Irish Chaplaincy. She was given assistance in arranging the funeral; the visits to her were increased; and she was helped to link back into the community. Nowadays she is very settled and attends a day centre four days a week. But she says she gets a bit lonely at the weekends and she still has a regular Chaplaincy visitor. What's more, the Chaplaincy arranged each year for Mamie to travel to Ireland to visit her sisters, both in their nineties; with somebody accompanying her to the airport and ensuring she has the support she needs when travelling. Mamie was able to go on such a trip a few months before one of her sisters passed away, and she was so pleased to have seen her before she died.

Mamie has also asked that we arrange her funeral when she dies and she will be buried in London with her Nicholas. Mamie's niece in Ireland told us, 'It is so lovely she is supported by the Chaplaincy. You are her family over there. Thank you so much.'

There are 20,000 elderly Irish living alone in London, according to the 2011 Census, and some of those we visit are not so willing to talk about their early lives; it's too painful. But what always strikes me is how grateful each person is for their visits from the Irish Chaplaincy, to have someone who comes regularly to sit with them and chat. 'I can't praise these people highly enough', and 'I don't know what I would have done without them', were two comments made during that day of visits. Sean, who sadly died in 2020 at the age of seventy-eight, said of his Chaplaincy visitor Pat, a fellow Dubliner, 'Pat is fantastic; I love his visits.' And Mamie has said, 'I would have gone downhill without the Chaplaincy. Now I'm enjoying life again and getting out.'

'Keep up the great work', was Alan's encouraging message to us the following day, and we have every intention of doing so. And the final comment from Mamie as we were saying our goodbyes: 'Make sure they send a bishop next time!'

Mamie's dream was to come true in 2019 when, thanks again to help from the Irish Chaplaincy Seniors' Project, she went on the Westminster Diocesan pilgrimage to Lourdes, a long-held wish. There is a photo of her outside the basilica in Lourdes, smiling broadly, with Vincent Nichols, Cardinal Archbishop of Westminster.

17. (I AIN'T GOT NO) BARMOUTH BLUES

Which is most beautiful, the Connemara coast or Cardigan Bay? I was discussing this with Chris, a Traveller from Galway, as we stood on the seafront at Barmouth. Barmouth is the little seaside town in North Wales where I spend a week every August, staying in the same place with the same group of people.

It all began in 2000. It was a millennium reunion for people who had met in the 1980s at the Sheffield University Catholic Chaplaincy and SVP (St Vincent de Paul Society). Our student SVP group was involved in various kinds of visiting, including to a geriatric hospital and a cancer hospital; and we also organised parties for the children of Travellers. Those were *very* lively affairs, and before I started at the Irish Chaplaincy it had been my sole contact with the world of Travellers. I especially enjoyed my weekly visits to the elderly, most of whom were living in various stages of dementia. It was perhaps the first insight for me that in any kind of social outreach the person supposedly giving seems in fact to be receiving at least as much. Also important for me was to be doing that in a faith context. Our SVP group would meet each week to pray together and to talk about how the visits had gone. It set the direction for what I was to do in my life: later joining a L'Arche community, and then coming to the Irish Chaplaincy.

Deep friendships had been formed (and some marriages made) at Sheffield, and the Barmouth week was a hit from the start, and with both old and young. The core of the group has been several couples, and our children in turn have developed close bonds with the other children that they saw from year to year. We're fortunate to be able to stay in the big Jesuit Holiday House, which has views of the steep, sheep-filled hills to the back, and the spectacular Cardigan Bay to the front. It even has a sandy beach. As long as the tide is out!

It is a sizeable group that gathers there, although it's becoming a bit smaller now as some of the now adult 'children' are unable to come. Part of the beauty of it is that both the group and the routines evolve a bit as the years go by but certain traditions remain the same. A different family cooks in the evening; there's an early morning running and swimming group, which is always one of my favourite bits of the week; and we have a time of prayer each day. For the first few years this took the form of a child-friendly Catholic Mass; then it became an ecumenical service; and for the last couple of years we've had a simple Taizé-style prayer in the evening around the dining-table. Like any group we need to adapt in order to survive and thrive.

Another great Barmouth tradition is the entertainment evening at the end of the week. For many years this was called a Talent Show, until some of the 'children' (by now young adults) thought this sounded too childish! I rebranded it as a Concert Night and the same things happened as before (people displaying their talents through music, word or dance) but everyone was happy to come. A couple of years ago I renamed it again, so that our special evening is now called the Barmouth Open Mic Night. It's as wonderful and fun and inspiring as ever. A new favourite is the 'Eddie Stobart Song', and this comes alongside old crowd pleasers such as '500 Miles' and Chris de Burgh's 70s classic 'Patricia the Stripper', complete with dance and actions from the men and boys. That one always brings the house down. And I always do a song I wrote some years ago following our week there: '(I

Ain't got no) Barmouth Blues'. I'm incredibly touched to see that some of the group now know the lyrics by heart and are singing along.

It was when I was out for the morning run that I met Chris from Galway. He had just emerged from his (illegally parked!) mobile home as I was warming down and preparing to face the waves, and we had got chatting. He invited me in for a coffee and it was tempting to talk more but I said I had to get into the sea for my swim and then get back for a shower. And the most beautiful out of the Connemara coast and Cardigan Bay? I'll sit on the fence and say that both are utterly stunning. I'm lucky to go back year after year to sit and look at and to walk, run and cycle alongside Cardigan Bay. And I would be returning to the Connemara coast later that year prior to going to Mayo for the sponsored Emigrants Walk with Alan Brogan to raise money for the Irish Chaplaincy Seniors' Project.

(I Ain't got no) Barmouth Blues

There's a big old house overlooking the sea
With hills at the back and the beach not far away
And every single year we gather in the month of August
There's a rota for the cooking and we eat real fine
A banquet in the evening and a glass of wine
Then we sit around and catch up on the news from the past
  year

In the early morning there's a running group
We jog along the beach then we jump in the soup
It's fun but it sure is cold in the Atlantic ocean
Back for a shower and a cup of tea
And the big Barmouth breakfast made by Rosie
Later we gather in the chapel for an original liturgy

LOOKING AHEAD WITH HOPE

Chorus
Well I ain't got no Barmouth blues
If I want a summer hol. there's no other place I'll choose
I like to hang out with my friends with whom I'm growing
old and grey
No, I ain't got no Barmouth blues
And I don't want no Caribbean cruise
I'll spend my days just sitting looking out at that bay

Well, we go to the beach if the weather is hot
We go to the beach even if it's not
Then we run up the hill to the house to the hot showers
On the final night there's a talent show
We have to do '500 miles' before we can go
Then the books come out and we sing till the early hours

Well I ain't got no Barmouth blues …

18. THE POPE IN IRELAND

I was in Dublin in August 2018 for the World Meeting of Families, attended by Pope Francis, and was touched and inspired by the whole occasion. The positive and joyful atmosphere around the various events was a welcome tonic and a sign of hope for a Church which, especially in Ireland, has taken a bit of a bashing in recent times.

I was staying with the Columbans, a missionary order that I had first got to know in Seoul when spending a year there. They were a great bunch of mainly Irish priests who had been in Korea for many years and they were full of stories that they loved to regale me with. And it was when the Irish Catholic bishops sent nine Columban priests to England in 1957 to minister to Irish emigrants like my parents that the Irish Chaplaincy was founded. In my first weeks at the Chaplaincy I was asked by several people if I was related to Bobby Gilmore, the Columban who had been Director of the Chaplaincy in the 70s and 80s. 'Not that I'm aware of,' was my usual response. But it turned out that Bobby had known my dad in Galway and even remembered him leaving in 1949. And he explained to me how my dad used to help with the hay-making on his (Bobby's) auntie's farm; and that just the other day his brother had been speaking with my aunty Nellie near Glenamaddy. And it turns out as well that Bobby and I may indeed be distantly related!

There was a lovely group of people from Chile who were also staying with the Columbans in Co. Meath and I travelled in with them on the Friday to the RDS exhibition halls in Dublin on a little coach they had hired. Denny, a Columban who had lived in Chile, led us in prayer and song in Spanish and English, having told us when we set off, 'This is not a tourist bus, this is a pilgrim bus!' After a long but very good day meeting interesting people from all over the world, I was pleased to be invited to join Denny, the Chileans and a couple of Korean Columbans for food and wine. I was on the coach with the group again on the Saturday to go to the 'Festival of Families' at Croke Park. It was a fantastic concert, the highlight for me being the sight and sound of 500 Irish dancers on the stage and around the pitch. As the woman next to me said, 'That must be the biggest Riverdance in history!' Before going to the stadium I'd wandered down to O'Connell Street where I chanced upon the arrival of the popemobile, and took a photo in which Francis seemed to be waving straight at me! I also happened to get interviewed for Ulster TV and gave quite a surprise to my aunties in Newry later that day when I suddenly appeared on the evening news!

On Sunday it was the papal Mass in Phoenix Park and I almost decided not to go after waking up to the sound of pouring rain. 'What's the point of walking for miles in the rain and standing soaked in a field for hours,' I'd asked myself. I travelled in with Tommy, a Columban who has lived in Beijing for many years and who was good company. We walked the few miles to and through the park with a couple we'd met on the bus and with the thousands of others going along the traffic-free streets. We got chatting to Miranda from Singapore and I mentioned the sole person I know in Singapore, a woman called Edwina who had been a fantastic and wise retreat guide of mine some years before at St Beuno's in Wales, and it turned out that she and Miranda were good friends! It really did feel like a pilgrimage and I was glad I hadn't stayed at home.

It was another joyful and uplifting celebration. And especially moving was the Penitential Rite, which is usually a set prayer at the start of the Mass: a kind of 'saying sorry' prayer. Francis, following his meeting the previous day with eight victims of abuse, read out in place of the set prayer a handwritten declaration of apology for all those who had been abused by ministers of the Church, and for the inexcusable cover-ups of those in leadership. He ended each sentence with the words, 'Forgive us'.

Ireland is certainly a very different country to that visited by Pope John Paul II in 1979, and the Catholic Church will need to make a slow and painful journey to regain the trust which has been shattered by multiple instances of abuse and cover-ups; also to look at what systemic changes need to be made to ensure both that past mistakes are not repeated, and that the Church can become more inclusive and a relevant force for good in today's world. Before the Pope's visit I was wondering if the Catholic Church in Ireland could ever recover from all that had happened. But having been there in Dublin to celebrate much of what is good in the Church, also to witness the head of the Catholic Church being truly humble and repentant, I had renewed hope. And it was interesting to look at the newspaper stands at the airport before flying home. Every single Irish paper had on its front page a picture of the Pope. And nearly every one of them had printed those words spoken so powerfully by Francis in Phoenix Park: 'Forgive us'. Saying sorry is not enough in itself, and contrition needs to be accompanied by concrete actions. But recognising the hurt that has been caused and taking full responsibility is important. Our world needs more than ever people who can dare to give hope to those in despair, comfort to those in pain, and to be a voice for the voiceless.

Like any human institution there are elements that are undesirable in the Church, but there is also tremendous good. I witnessed some of that good in my few days in Dublin: meeting many committed and faithful people at all levels of the Church, who are doing great work in their respective fields and proclaiming a message of compassion and hope to a broken world. And in proclaiming this message we can perhaps remember the words of the famous saint from whom our current Pope took his name, Francis of Assisi, and who is said to have said: 'Preach the gospel at all times, and if necessary, use words.'

19. CARITAS AT VILLA PALAZZOLA

I get the chance through my work to meet a lot of great people, in some interesting places, and the Caritas Leadership Week near Rome organised by CSAN (Caritas Social Action Network), of which Irish Chaplaincy is a part, did not disappoint. We were a group of fifty, representing a range of Catholic charities and dioceses in England and Wales, staying at Villa Palazzola, a thirteenth-century Cistercian monastery perched above a volcanic lake, Lago di Albano, and, according to the website, 'Rome's best kept secret'.

From the garden terrace at the Villa, where pre-dinner drinks were served in the evening, the view is vast and truly breath-taking. On the opposite side of the lake can be seen the twin towers of Castel Gandolfo, the summer papal residence. At least it used to be. The taxi driver who drove me up from the station was complaining that Pope Francis, who doesn't take holidays, has never visited, which has wrecked the local economy! Beyond Castel Gandolfo can be seen, in the distance, the urban sprawl of Rome; and further still on a clear day the bright blue of the Mediterranean. I loved to stand on that terrace at various times of the day and to behold the subtly changing vista and colours. The sunsets over the lake were especially stunning.

For me, a key element of such events will always be meeting people and building relationships, and I was touched and inspired by those I met. I could see how everybody in the group was enjoying encountering one another on a very human level, and getting a sense of being part of something greater than ourselves and our own organisation. The nice location helped with that; also being well cared for, with good food and a choice of wines with every meal. Occasionally I resisted the large carafes of wine on offer but mostly I didn't! And there was also a swimming pool, which I had been particularly looking forward to using. I managed four swims during the meeting, also three runs through the woods that circle the lake. It was fun to swim and run with others: there are some very sporty types in the Caritas family!

There were echoes for me of one particular L'Arche Directors week which was held in the North of Scotland (and, as with the Caritas gathering, the building of relationships was also a fundamental aspect of those events). We usually stayed, quite simply and cheaply, in convents or retreat houses. But Robin, who was then leader of L'Arche Inverness, and who broke the mould in every way, had booked us into a Highland hotel, complete with trampoline, swimming pool, and ... hot tub. I can really recommend a good bounce on the trampoline after a heavy meeting, or a few lengths of the pool. And late in the evening a group of us would luxuriate in the hot tub, being served cold beers by a young Latvian waiter! I thought I had gone to heaven.

In common with those L'Arche meetings, another central element of the Caritas week was prayer and liturgy. Amongst the group were four of the loveliest and most down to earth priests, also a deacon, and they led us in a daily celebration of Mass, and in the Morning (7.15 a.m.!) and Evening prayer of the Church. One morning the Mass was in the crypt of St Peter's, in front of the tomb of St Peter; and the following day it was with the bishops of England and Wales in the magnificent basilica of St Paul's Outside the Walls, and which included a final prayer at the tomb of St Paul.

And there was music! I found a guitar in the house and one evening after the bar had opened, I got together with Sean who had a collection of tin whistles and recorders, having worked as a professional musician before joining Caritas. What a session that was! We spent about two hours singing mainly Irish songs, some of which I hadn't sung in over twenty years but somehow could still remember the words to. Being a mainly Catholic group, a lot of people had Irish roots and there was no shortage of either requests for yet another Irish song or people joining in. Then on the final night Sean compered a musical evening during which several people did turns. One of my favourite pieces was a music hall song called 'Light fingered Freddy' which is from a Salvation Army musical. I never knew such a thing existed! Yes, one of the CSAN directors, Garry, is a salvationist, and what a great guy he is. He runs as well!

We were not just eating, drinking, singing, swimming and praying. There was excellent input, besides two trips into Rome to meet different groups, and to have lunch with the British Ambassador to the Vatican. The main speaker was Kerry Robinson, who founded 'Leadership Roundtable' based in Washington DC. She was particularly eloquent on the urgent need for the Catholic Church to harness the gifts of women in leadership at all levels. I was excited when Kerry mentioned Henri Nouwen, the Dutch priest who had been a member of L'Arche in Toronto, and of how he had encouraged us to be people of joy and gratitude. This was in the context of fundraising which was one of the themes of the week and I later shared with the group something Henri has once said in a talk about fundraising: 'When we ask people for money we shouldn't be embarrassed or apologetic; we should say, "It is my pleasure to invite you to share in our mission!"'

I left Villa Palazzola inspired and encouraged, and grateful for having made some lovely new connections with people. And soon after Rome I was heading off again to Ireland. What a journey that turned out to be ...

20. FROM MAYNOOTH TO MAYO ... TRAVELS IN IRELAND

Mass with the Irish Catholic Bishops' Conference in the magnificent St Patrick's Chapel at Maynooth was the start of a five-night trip that would take me across Ireland, up a holy mountain, and finishing with a fundraising walk with two famous Gaelic footballers and a bishop, amongst others.

The Mass at Maynooth was very moving, thanks in part to the beautiful singing in harmonies of the male/female choir, including a soloist with the voice of an angel, and as always on such occasions there was a sumptuous meal laid on afterwards in the grand dining-room (one of the contenders, I was told, for the Hogwarts film set). Archbishop Diarmuid Martin of Dublin gave thanks in his speech for those who had made the recent World Meeting of Families such a success and spoke of his hope that much fruit could come from that.

After spending the night with friends in Kildare I drove up to Northern Ireland to my mum's hometown of Newry, where we had gone on family holidays. Going along the M1 from the South into the North it is possible to not notice that you've crossed any kind of border, except for a sign informing people that distances are now measured in miles, not kilometres. Army checkpoints are a long distant childhood memory, and I prayed that Brexit would not undo any of the incredible work that has been done to achieve such a 'soft' border. I had a lovely visit in Newry with aunties, one uncle and even, by chance, with a cousin I'd last seen when she was thirteen. Martina is now forty-eight and she's the daughter of my Uncle Pat who gets a mention elsewhere in this book. A lot of tea was drunk and a lot of food was consumed. I learnt a long time ago that saying no is futile! ('Ah, go on, have another cup/slice/plate …').

From Newry I drove back towards Dublin and then headed West, where I ended up in Galway City. Going out there in the evening I got caught between hearing live music and watching football (it was a Champions League night!) and ended up doing neither very satisfactorily. But I did enjoy a group of seven street musicians doing an eclectic mix of songs on a variety of instruments. When out for my walk the following morning, I chanced upon a 7.20 a.m. Mass in the Dominican church by the harbour, after which I was ready in body and spirit for my full Irish breakfast. I was then on the road north from the city towards Glenamaddy, near which my dad was born and raised. I was visiting my Aunty Nellie who is the last surviving member of the family there. It was only the second time we had met and the first time we had actually spoken: a long story, but one with a happy and a healing ending. We chatted easily with one another, and the bountiful tea and cake was followed by a walk across a couple of fields to see the old croft house where dad was born. It's a single-story dwelling, now used for storage, with a central kitchen area and two small rooms either side. And which was home to a family of seven. I was happy to finally see the house, so too the graveyard where my paternal grandparents are buried, both of them having died before I was born.

Leaving Lisheen, the tiny village where Nellie lives, I just about managed to find my way back along the narrow country lanes to Glenamaddy for a quick look at the town and at the pub on the crossroads where I'd been present some years before for a truly unforgettable auction of some land that I'd ended up with a small stake in. And to this day, I own a share in a strip of bogland in County Galway that nobody wanted to buy! My destination was Clifden over on the coast, and, just as I had done on my previous trip to Galway, I stopped off at Cong, the '*Quiet Man*' village. It was raining so I didn't hang around. I took a quick photo of the statue of John Wayne carrying Maureen O'Hara and then carried on around the stunning shoreline of Lough Corrib. Clifden is especially known for its music and on my last visit every one of the many pubs was packed and even the pavements outside. The village was eerily quiet with it being 'off season' but I still managed to find a good three-piece band in Griffins Bar, where I was one of the few people present who was not American!

The next day I was driving through the vast, rugged, beautiful wilderness of Connemara, at times being the only car for miles around. I was going to Croagh Patrick, the Holy Mountain, at the top of which (Ireland's highest point) St Patrick is said to have fasted for forty days and from where he banished the snakes from Ireland. It was my second ascent and, as with the first, I was lucky with the weather and had spectacular views down over the estuary going out into the Atlantic, and the little islets dotted about. I met a lot of interesting people on the way: a couple of Irish guys who were walking up 'The Reek' for the thirty-fifth time, an Australian woman whose family had come from Mayo, and a young French couple who shared their coffee with me at the top. Many people who walk Croagh Patrick do so in a spirit of penitence; some even walk it barefoot. I would say that I was doing it more in a spirit of thanksgiving.

I met up in Westport with some of the guys from the Irish Chaplaincy who were also taking part in the Sponsored Emigrants' Walk, to raise money for our Seniors' Project. We gathered the following day at Mulranny in Mayo at the start of the Great Western Greenway, with several people having made the long drive over from Dublin. There was Alan

Brogan together with his father Bernard Snr, both of whom had won All-Ireland titles with Dublin; there was Bishop John Kirby who at that time chaired the Irish Episcopal Council for Emigrants; there were friends from Maynooth, including a very welcome car with food supplies driven by Harry; and there was a group of staff and volunteers and friends from the Chaplaincy. Again, we were blessed with the weather for the seventeen kilometre walk to Newport and it was a wonderful occasion, for which we were grateful to everybody who helped make it happen and to everyone who gave their support.

For our final evening in Westport we went to Matt Molloy's (he of 'Chieftans' fame), which is a quite remarkable labyrinth of a place: a series of rooms, all packed with people, ending in a courtyard space at the back where there was a fantastic four-piece in full flow. From traditional Irish they went very eclectic in the series of encores ('Ah go on, just one more…'), which included a great version of The Undertones' classic 'Teenage Kicks', with the fiddle player doing the guitar solo bit. As I was telling people all around me, I had sung that song at my wedding wearing a pink suit! Let me explain: Yim Soon and I had changed into traditional Korean dress for the reception, and the colour in fashion that year happened to be pink, so there's a wonderful picture in our wedding album of me in pink baggy trousers and a pink jacket playing guitar with the wedding band, and belting out 'Teenage Kicks'.

It was the cherry on the icing on the cake of a very special and blessed few days in Ireland.

21. THE WORLD IS A HANDKERCHIEF

Yim Soon and I were staying with our friends Paul and Moira near Liverpool and Paul was telling us about his voluntary work as Chair of the St Bart's & Friends Community Sponsorship Scheme, by which careful preparations are made for the welcome of a Syrian refugee family into a parish. He mentioned the excellent input the group had received from Sean Ryan of Caritas Salford who is the national lead for the scheme. 'Sean the musician?' I asked. It was indeed the same Sean that I had been in Rome with a few weeks previously for the Caritas Leadership Week and with whom I'd enjoyed a couple of great sessions of music.

Paul went on to tell us about the time he was staying on a remote Thai island and had overheard a man with a Tyrone accent. It turned out that he was from Coalisland, like Paul, and asked if Paul was related to Charlie Devlin the singer. 'He's my dad,' replied Paul. I reminded Paul of the time in 1985 when he had met an even more famous son of Coalisland, Dennis Taylor. Paul spotted Dennis coming out of Mass at St Marie's Cathedral in the centre of Sheffield, where he and Moira and I were students at the time and whose Crucible Theatre was, as it still is, the home of the World Snooker Championship. It was the week before the epic final in which Dennis came back from 7-0 down to defeat Steve Davis. I remember at the time Paul telling me that he went up to him and said, 'You're Dennis Taylor; you're from Coalisland,' and Mr Taylor not being too impressed until Paul said that he too was a native of the town. Paul recalled then that in 2010 he was at a dinner in Manchester where Dennis Taylor was to be the guest speaker. They ended up sitting near one another and Paul introduced himself and spoke of the encounter outside the Cathedral twenty-five years before. Dennis was touched by that and began his speech (which was mainly about the 1985 final) by mentioning that he was happy to have just met somebody from his hometown who he had also spoken to briefly just before that final.

I love these constant reminders that we are surely far more connected to one another than we could ever imagine. One of many wonderful encounters I had when walking on the Camino to Santiago in Spain was with a Spanish man called Rodrigo ('Call me Rod!'). He spoke very good English, albeit with a strong Spanish accent, and I was sure that I could hear a bit of Irish in there. I asked him how he had learnt English and he replied that he'd been married to an Irish woman for forty years. 'Where in Ireland is your wife from?' I asked. 'The North.' 'Where in the North?' 'County Down.' 'Where in County Down?' 'Newry.' I explained that my mum was from Newry and when I bumped into Rod again the next day he told me that he'd called his wife and she knew my Uncle Pat who had been a butcher in the town. Soon after this I got chatting to another man who wasn't actually walking the Camino. He was a local out for a walk and I'd only met him due to taking a big detour from the official route. I managed with my limited Spanish to tell him the story of Rodrigo, his wife and Uncle Pat and he said to me, 'El mundo es un pañuelo,' the world is a handkerchief. In my first year at the Irish Chaplaincy I got talking to a guy called Rory at a conference whose dad was from Newry and after investigation it emerged that he too knew Uncle Pat. When I reported this to mum she said, 'Ah, sure the whole town knows Pat!'

And returning to the Caritas week in Rome where I met and made music with the aforementioned Sean Ryan. After running one day with Celia, another member of the group, I'd spoken about doing the London Marathon in 2009 for Jesuit Missions, and she told me that her brother had also run for Jesuit Missions around about that time. When I got home after the meeting and checked the names on my JM team vest it turned out that I had indeed run with Ged, the brother of Celia. I sent her a message to let her know and she replied, 'What a wonderful and small world it is.'

Our world is indeed a handkerchief, as that Spanish man told me, and a beautifully woven one. And what treasures await us sometimes when we decide to take a detour.

22. DENISE RIGDEN RIP

St Mildred's Church in Canterbury was packed full for a celebration of the life of a great friend of mine, Denise Rigden. And in honour of a woman who almost every day wore party dresses, fancy shoes and a flower in her hair, the invitation had been for us to dress as if coming to a wedding.

Denise was a local woman, born in Whitstable in 1947, and her beloved family were there at the funeral, together with many past and present members of L'Arche, where Denise had lived since 1999, making her home at 'Rainbow', one of the L'Arche houses in Canterbury. It was at Rainbow the evening before that lots of Denise's family and friends had gathered to see the body and to pray, sing and tell stories, a L'Arche tradition. Tuuliki told of how she and Denise had been part of a holiday group to Scotland one year and when Denise's (very heavy) suitcase was opened at the destination it was found to be completely filled with magazines. They were waiting to be cut up, one of Denise's favourite past-times! James told of how it had been discovered after several years that Denise had been bringing a cup of tea every morning to Yvonne, one of her housemates. It was only found out when Yvonne finally complained about being woken up each day at 5 a.m.! It showed the very caring side of Denise, which expressed itself even in her dying days when she was constantly asking about the 'ill' lady in her hospital ward.

I was very fond of Denise. During the years when I was based in the L'Arche offices in Barfreston near Dover we didn't see one another very often but whenever we did, Denise would shriek with delight. I was also one of only two men in the world, the other being her brother-in-law Mike, that she called by their actual name. Most other men were referred to as John, or occasionally by a nickname. Denise's niece Fiona shared at the funeral how her then boyfriend Phil was given the name 'tall boy'. And that was what Denise had always called him! I was very touched whenever Denise called me by my name, and she would often follow it up with a request, partly made in very effusive sign language, to come to my house for a cup of tea. How could I refuse! We had a little routine going over the years: drive to my house, tea and cake, then sometimes watch *Mamma Mia!*. What fun we had.

I was delighted to be asked to join the music group at the funeral, and we made a great sound that Denise would have loved. And I was honoured to be invited to sing a song I'd written for Denise one year for her birthday: 'When I See Your Face'. The chorus is as follows:

> I get a happy feeling inside whenever I see your face
> Your look of joy when I appear, it's like a warm embrace
> You don't need to speak at all but if my name you say
> It never fails to make me smile and to brighten up my day[

There were some unexpected and amazing connections during the day. As Yim Soon and I were getting our car from the car park to drive to the crematorium, who should we bump into but Martin, a man we had met the year before while walking on the Camino in Spain. And then at the crematorium how fitting it was for us to finish by singing 'I watch the sunrise'. I was reminded of an Irish Chaplaincy Staff Away Day that had taken place at the Sisters of Mercy Retirement community in Clacton-on-Sea. One of our lovely volunteers, Moira, is a member of that congregation and had warmly welcomed us there, fed us abundantly, and introduced us to some of the elderly sisters. We ended the day by celebrating Mass together in their beautiful chapel and I'd chosen as the final hymn 'I watch the sunrise'. It was explained to me afterwards that the song had been written at that very place by John Glynn when he'd been convalescing and had been able to look out at the sea and the sky in the various times of the day. And as we think of Denise and of all our loved ones who have died, the line in the last verse of the song about the sunset fading away is especially poignant.

23. McCOOL TRAD
AT HMP CHELMSFORD

The band were in full swing when I arrived in the prison chapel: the two fiddle players and two accordionists of McCool Trad making a lovely sound with their gentle Irish jigs.

Four of us from the Irish Chaplaincy were there to join the lovely Sister P., Merryl and Fr Paul of the prison Chaplaincy team for the Traveller Forum at HMP Chelmsford. The last time I attended, it had been a 'lively' occasion to say the least, and it was almost impossible for those addressing the group to make themselves heard over the shouting and antics from one or two of those present. It's hardly surprising that the guys coming to the forum should be so chatty and full of energy. Many are on twenty-three hour 'bang up'. Also, it might be the first time in ages they have seen a mate from a different wing.

The music created a pleasant atmosphere and the group seemed more peaceful and relaxed than on previous occasions. I had some touching conversations with several of the guys, and I ended up eating with four English Gypsies who had joined the gathering of mainly Irish Travellers. Three of those were brothers. The other had never met them before but it turned out that he knew their grandfather and as they spoke there were all kinds of other connections that emerged. We were all appreciative of the company and the good food: bacon, cabbage and potatoes. Somebody noticed that I didn't have a plastic knife and kindly went to fetch one for me. When it was announced that there were seconds, there was a mass dash to the servers, and I wondered how the men could eat two big plates of hot food so soon after lunch. Later it was explained to me what lunch consists of: a bag delivered to the cell containing a roll, a packet of crisps, a Penguin, a piece of fruit (which, apparently, is not necessarily eaten), and, for the following day's breakfast, a 30g packet of cereal and a carton of milk (with no fridge to keep it in). Prisons in the UK are really not the holiday camps portrayed in some sections of the media, especially since they have just £1.87 per prisoner per day to spend on food.

The Traveller Forum was a truly special occasion in every way, and there followed dessert, which was sticky toffee pudding and custard which I ate with a father and son, and the son's father-in-law! At the previous event I attended there had also been a father and son, and it's tragic how for some Traveller families this is the only life they know.

There was more music from McCool Trad, including the mournful and beautiful 'Ashokan Farewell'. I looked around the room. A few people were still chatting but most were sitting in silence, transfixed by the music. It was a powerful moment of togetherness before we had to say our goodbyes. I asked one of the three brothers what the rest of his day was looking like. 'Bang up till tomorrow,' he said. And then he looked me in the eyes and said, 'Thanks for coming.'

For a couple of hours we'd been fellow human beings, enjoying good food and music and one another's company. And as I chatted to the band on the way out I told them what a difference their music had made. They were profoundly moved by the experience, just as I had been the first time I played in a prison. I couldn't wait for the next Traveller event, the 'Christmas special' at Wormwood Scrubs.

24. BACON AND CABBAGE (AND HOW I CAME TO LIKE IT)

It's funny how I've come to like bacon and cabbage from eating it in prison! I couldn't stand it as a child. My dad's family in Galway used to send us occasionally a big chunk of bacon in a brown paper parcel and it must have taken a few days by post so that when it was unwrapped the smell was overpowering. It was duly cooked with cabbage and potatoes and enjoyed as a special 'taste of old Ireland' by mum and dad, while my sister and I wouldn't go near it.

My second pre-Christmas bacon and cabbage meal in a week, after Chelmsford, was at Wormwood Scrubs. There had been a particularly tasty bacon and cabbage stew at the Scrubs in March for our Irish Chaplaincy St Patrick's event. Some of the guys had complained that you shouldn't make bacon and cabbage into a stew but they ate it all the same. It really had been delicious, especially soaked up by soda bread, which for me will always evoke memories of childhood holidays in Ireland. This time it was the Irish Chaplaincy Christmas special and our amazing Breda, Ellena and Liz, with some volunteers and myself in tow, had pulled out all the stops. We had with us a dozen members of the Irish Elders' Choir; John and John from the Irish Embassy; and Sally from Irish Elderly Advice Network, with her wonderful daughter Nora who was directing the choir, playing fiddle along with Jaqui on flute and whistles and Billy on keyboards, *and* managing to get a substantial amount of audience participation. And there were people from several prison departments, including Sarah, the new Governor who, like everybody else there, was very appreciative of the work of the Irish Chaplaincy and of all who had helped with the event. I should say as well that getting even a couple of guests into a prison is not always a straightforward matter; to get almost twenty-five in is nothing short of miraculous.

After the choir and the musicians had performed for us, the food arrived. There's something very intimate and, I suppose, profoundly human, about sharing a meal, and, as said already, it's always for me a key part of these kind of events. And this meal was a true feast. Plates of bacon, cabbage and potatoes were served to us at our tables, followed by mince pies and, as usual, there was good banter. One of the guys gave me a (very welcome) second mince pie. 'Ah, go on,' he said, 'it's Christmas!'

Fully fed, we returned for some final songs from the choir, and there were repeated calls for, 'One more song!' For the grand finale Nora invited the men to come and join the choir. They were a bit shy at first but after one or two went up, lots more followed, and the sight of the Irish Elders' Choir in their emerald green tops surrounded by a sizeable group of (mainly young and mainly wearing grey) Traveller men, all belting out 'Dirty old Town' was, as one of the prison staff remarked to me, 'Magical'.

As the guys were getting ready to be brought back to the wings, one said to me, 'That was the highlight of the year.' It had to be one of the highlights for me too. And I never thought I'd say it, but I was looking forward to the next bacon and cabbage meal!

25. MEMORIES AND SONGS FROM A GRATEFUL GUEST

I first discovered the Monastery of the Holy Trinity at Crawley Down in Sussex in 1991 when seeking somewhere for a quiet weekend away from the busyness of the L'Arche house where I was living at the time. I had just started going out with the woman who was to become my wife and I remember using the telephone in the guest kitchen to share the news with my parents. That phone, out of action now for many years, still has for me a certain sacredness about it. As does everything in that simple kitchen. As does so much now, after many subsequent visits: the guest cloister and the orchard, the chapel and refectory, the woods and the walk down to the lake, occasionally frozen over in the depths of winter. There are other seasonal treats: the bluebells in April and, in May, the deliciously fragrant yellow azalea near the main gate; the apple blossom; the rich red of the sunset sky on a summer's evening. And there is also the stark, bare beauty of the tall trees in the winter. There is beauty to be found in every season.

I enjoy and appreciate the simple rituals in the refectory like the gathering of mugs for the second cup of tea at breakfast and the passing of the bread box for a second (or even third!) slice. And what pleasure to see a plate of little chocolates appear on feast days! Once, when I was setting off for Crawley Down, one of my children said to me, rather dismissively, 'Oh, is that the place where you get, like, one sweet at Christmas!'

LOOKING AHEAD WITH HOPE

When I was the father of young children, besides having a people-intensive day job, my visits to the monastery were one of the things that preserved my sanity, as well as nourishing my creative spirit. There is something healing and ordering and renewing about the monastic rhythm. And I have also tried to bring a little of the monastery into my own life. Each morning I sing Psalm 63 which is sung every day at the monastery at their 7 a.m. Lauds service, and I often say the Crawley Down grace to myself before meals.

For many years now one of my visits has been for a night or two at the end of Advent. I find this a wonderful still point in the, often frenetic, build up to Christmas, and I particularly look forward to the singing of 'O Come, O Come Emmanuel' at Lauds, with the adding on of a verse each morning. Once, arriving late in the day for my Advent stay, I made a very dramatic entrance when, thinking I knew my way around the guest cloister in the dark, I walked straight into one of the wooden posts. I was able to use this incident the following year in a Good Friday reflection at L'Arche to graphically illustrate the reply of a monk when asked what people did in monasteries: 'Oh, we fall down and we get up, we fall down and we get up, we fall down and we get up!' During my Advent stay another year I wrote a Christmas song, 'A Stable in Bethlehem', and finished an Advent song, 'A Light in the Darkness', based on some of my favourite bits from Isaiah, and the lyrics are below.

I am profoundly grateful to the community at Crawley Down for their constant warm welcome and for their faithfulness in preserving what has become for many a sacred place of rest and renewal.

A Light in the Darkness
All ears shall be opened, the blind have their sight
For the people in darkness have seen a great light
Their gladness is greater, their joy will increase
For a new King is coming to bring the world peace
Those living in shadow will no longer mourn
A sign has been given, a child will be born
Who'll soothe all our sorrow and banish our shame
Emmanuel- God with us- is his name

Prepare in the desert a highway
Be ready because on that day
The people shall see an incredible sight
God coming in our darkest night

To the Prince of Peace, Eternal Father we pray
For the justice, integrity that comes on that day
Sing and cry out, tell the good news to all
Wonder counsellor, mighty God: names we will call
A banquet of rich food, a feast of fine wine
On the mountain prepared for God's glory to shine
He'll bind up the broken hearts, wipe away tears
Joy will go with us, there'll be no more fears

Prepare in the desert …

26. BE THOU MY VISION

The decorations were down, the bare Christmas trees had been sent to the tip, and there were no more flashing fairy lights outside houses to brighten up my early morning walks. It was mid-January, it was already the third week back at work, and it was not always easy in those dark days to find motivation and meaning. And it's no wonder that many people begin at that time of year to book their summer holidays, with the lure of long sunny days 'away from it all'.

I couldn't even get motivated that January to make any new year's resolutions! I wasn't sure what I wanted from the year, or, for that matter, what I wanted to give. A few days before, I'd decided to get my act together and organise a couple of musical gatherings at my house. I'd had a good and creative two years at the Irish Chaplaincy up until that point but there hadn't been much time or energy left over for music so I planned to redress that a bit. Oh, and Yim Soon and I found cheap flights to Portugal for the end of April. We couldn't wait for the summer!

My little bit of light in the darkness came one day in the form of a ninety-two-year-old woman called Ellen who was originally from County Cork. I'd been visiting Ellen regularly for about a year and a half and we had a bit of a routine going. We'd have a chat over a cup of tea; then, as she was housebound so couldn't get out to church, we'd have a little communion service and some prayers; and we'd sing a song, usually 'Be Thou my Vision'. Ellen had been going downhill health-wise and her daughter Lorraine informed me in the December that she'd gone into hospital. I went over just before Christmas and she didn't recognise me at first, then her face lit up and she said, 'Oh, we pray together!' We did our usual communion service and sang 'Be Thou My Vision', and then she began to recite from memory a long litany of prayers to various saints, which must have been something recalled from her childhood. She had not done that before. It was very moving.

We receive a wide variety of calls at the Irish Chaplaincy from people who are Irish or of Irish heritage. The week before seeing Ellen I'd spoken to a woman who wanted help with preparing the funeral service for her Irish mother. I'd given some suggestions, including singing 'Be Thou my Vision', and wished her a wonderful celebration of the life of her mother and she was so grateful.

Ellen was barely conscious when I saw her that last time in the hospital, and Lorraine had already warned me that she wouldn't be going home and that this could be the final leg of the journey. I did what I'd always done on my visits to her. I sang 'Be Thou my Vision', and followed that with a mix of other Irish songs. I don't know what effect it had on Ellen, who slept throughout, but after a day, and indeed a month, in which I'd felt a little out of sorts, I suddenly found myself at peace through the intimate contact with that special woman.

Lorraine arrived whilst I was there, with her husband Paddy. We chatted a bit, then as I made my leave Lorraine looked me in the eyes and said, 'Eddie, thank you'. 'It's my pleasure,' I replied, and it really was. Lorraine called me a few days later to say that her mum had passed away peacefully.

27. SABBATICAL ADVENTURES

I often recall, in the dark days of January, a special trip that Yim Soon and I made in that month some years ago. I'd been fortunate to have been given a six-month sabbatical from L'Arche after finishing a nine-year stint as Community Leader, and our first evening in Tallinn, near the end of the sabbatical, contained something of the essence of those six months: rich, often unexpected encounters; interesting adventures; blessings received. We were trudging through the deep snow towards the city centre and found ourselves walking past a Japanese shop, which seemed rather incongruous on a residential street in Estonia. The two young Japanese men inside saw us and called us in and gave us green tea and we chatted warmly about what had brought us all there. And equally unexpected was the news that there was a Korean restaurant just five minutes' walk away. Our first meal, then, in Tallinn was Korean and when I remarked to the owner, in Korean, that I was surprised to find him there, he replied, 'I'm more surprised to find someone from England in Estonia speaking Korean!' Later in the evening we walked around the exquisite old town; then, through chatting with some locals, found the best blues bar in Tallinn and had a long conversation with a friend of the singer who was performing that night.

The sabbatical had kicked off the previous August with the first of many special little trips, this one with the whole family to an Olympic football match between South Korea and Switzerland in my hometown of Coventry. Some of the locals were saying it was the best football ever seen at the Ricoh Arena! I had been determined to make the most of the six months away, to catch up on family and old friends and to do some of the things I'd always dreamed of doing. One of those things was spending some time in a French L'Arche community. I chose La Vallée in the Southeast of the country, since the Community Leader at that time was my friend Pat who I used to meet each year in the Alps. It was a privilege to spend a couple of weeks living in one of the houses and working in the craft workshop and there was much kindness towards me and some very special moments. One of my favourites was watching with the people in the house a World Cup match between France and Finland. There was a lovely old lady there called Paulette and she said she wanted to stay up to see the game. Anita the House Leader said, 'I didn't know you liked football, Paulette!' '*Ah, oui*', she replied. We all sat through the match and at the end as the teams were leaving the pitch Paulette said, 'So which one was France?'

After La Vallée I spent a blissful week in silence at Taizé, an inter-denominational monastic community, before finishing off my French adventure with two nights in Paris staying with the very impressive Simon of Cyrene community that supports people who have had brain injuries as adults, and whose director Maxime I'd met at a L'Arche event. As with everywhere else I'd been, I received a warm welcome and met some great people.

I was back in France in the October, this time with Yim Soon on a long car journey down to the south west. It included a visit to Lourdes, where Yim Soon had always wanted to go; and to Robin (he of the Highland hot tub!) and his family in L'Arche Agen, near Toulouse. The final leg of the journey was L'Arche Ambleteuse, near Boulogne, where we saw David Wilson, one of the priests who had married us twenty years before. That was a special trip. As was the next one ... to Ireland. We stayed at L'Arche in Belfast, a long-held dream of mine, and there was one utterly unforgettable, besides song-inspiring, evening at Fibber McGees, a live music bar, which we spent with three Guinness-loving Swedes and a couple from County Tyrone. We had a wonderful day with the wonderful Maria, who Yim Soon and I had first met on a L'Arche training week in 1991. Maria, who founded L'Arche Belfast and for whom everything is possible, said one morning, 'Let's go to Corrymeela,' knowing that I'd always wanted to visit this centre of peace and reconciliation on the beautiful North Antrim coast (and whose motto is 'together is better'). And that's where we went! The Ireland trip also enabled a first visit to family in Newry for twenty-seven years, and a day with friends in Dublin.

And then there was Estonia! Which came about when some of our lovely Estonian assistants at L'Arche had asked me the previous summer to go there on my sabbatical. Well, how could I say no! Yim Soon and I stayed at Maria Village, a community similar to L'Arche. But which L'Arche community has got a sauna? I have to say that the sauna experience is to be thoroughly recommended. And we did it the Estonian way: 100 degrees of heat, then rolling in the snow outside or jumping through an ice hole into a frozen pond, with the air temperature at -16 degrees. That was something I had *always* wanted to do.

I returned to L'Arche after those six months truly renewed.

28. CONCERT AT ST JAMES'S PICCADILLY

It all began with a cup of tea and a chat about fundraising.

I'd first got to know Lucy Winkett, rector of St James's Piccadilly, in 1992 when she spent six months at Cana, the L'Arche house where I was House Leader. Lucy describes this time at L'Arche as being one of her two strongest spiritual influences; the other being a month-long silent Ignatian retreat. We used to sing a bit in the evenings. Lucy would do Mary Black; I would do The Undertones. And she sang, very beautifully, at my wedding. I didn't see too much of her in the ensuing years but it was special for me to drive a carload of L'Arche members up to East London for Lucy's ordination as priest and later for her installation as a canon at St Paul's Cathedral. And I always loved hearing her on Radio 4's *Thought for the Day*, or reading an article she'd written.

I'd got in touch to tell Lucy I was now working in London, and we were having a cup of tea and a catch-up and got to talking about the various amounts of money we had to raise each year to keep our respective shows on the road. And she said with her usual infectious optimism, 'We can help you do some fundraising; you could do a concert in the church.' It seemed like a good idea at the time: a 'Celebration of Irish music, theatre, poetry and dancing in the week of St Brigid.' But then there was the reality of actually finding musicians, actors, poets and dancers, and ensuring that we didn't end up losing money from the event rather than gaining it! I was worried I'd bitten off more than I could chew. I was reassured by Paul, one of our wonderful team at the Irish Chaplaincy, and decided to take a step in faith, and thanks to the kindness and support of many people things just fell into place. I spoke to Nora who directs both the Irish Elders' Choir and Irish Elders' Theatre and she was only too happy to help. Yes, the choir would sing for us again; and yes, Elders' theatre would write and perform a play about St Brigid, patron saint of the Irish Chaplaincy. And she would involve Jaqui and Billy, two of her talented musician friends who had played at our memorable Christmas concert in Wormwood Scrubs prison.

I found poets. There was Gerry, Gerry and Rory from the Chaplaincy; plus Anton Thompson- McCormick who had performed for us before, both at the Irish Embassy and in a prison, and who, on the night, sang the beautifully haunting 'Siúil a Rún'.

I still needed a kind of 'headline' act. I'd been at a concert at the London Irish Centre and had been impressed by the Byrne-Whelehan Family Band. A few days after that I was at an Embassy event and the first person I bumped into was Eilish Byrne-Whelehan who I'd met there before. I thought, 'This is fate!' I explained about the concert and Eilish said she'd be delighted to help. She could bring twenty musicians from the Feíth and Cheoíl School of Music, including harps and dancers! We also found a sponsor, Derek Platt of Platt Reilly (partition and ceiling experts). We were in business!

The concert duly took place at the end of January 2019. We hoped we might get a hundred people attending: there were 200 on the night and it was the most wonderful evening. Lucy did a couple of Mary Black songs, including my favourite 'Once in a very blue moon'. And I had the privilege of finishing the evening with a few songs, including my setting of 'St Patrick's Breastplate'. We were all agreed that we really had to do it again the following year …

29. YOU'RE ONLY
FIFTY-FOUR ONCE

I don't usually do much for my birthday but in 2019 I decided to push the boat out.

When, in the dark days of January, I'd planned a couple of musical gatherings at my house, Yim Soon had suggested that one of them be close to my birthday. The guest list began quite small but grew to the point where I wasn't sure we'd have enough places for people to sit. And in the couple of hours before everyone arrived, I was hastily assembling some IKEA stools that we'd bought years previously. I'd also received a few days beforehand an email from Haesook, a lovely Korean woman I'd worked with at L'Arche, and who I hadn't seen since I'd left two years previously. She had subsequently gone to L'Arche in Brisbane: where, she informed me, L'Arche shares an office with the Irish Chaplaincy in Australia! Haesook was going to be in Canterbury for a few days and wondered if we could meet up. By happy coincidence it was when I was having my gathering, and she was able to come. It was great to see her again, and I was incredibly touched when she told me she had read every single one of my blogs since they started, so that when I began to tell her I'd just organised a concert in London she said, 'Yes, I know, I read the blog!'

The guests were people I'd got to know through my thirty-one years in Canterbury: some at L'Arche; some through the children; others at church; some a combination of these. It was a wonderfully international group (Korean, French, German, British, Anglo-Irish), and Yim Soon had prepared a sumptuous Korean meal. I'd offered to help but she wouldn't let me in the kitchen; and anyway, I was busy with my IKEA stools! We ate, we drank, and then we sang. I kicked it off with a couple of easy singalongs, then there was a request from my then four-year-old godson Carlos for 'Jubilee Blues'. It's a song I wrote for a CD, 'The Jubilee Sessions', which was recorded in 2014 to mark the 50th anniversary of L'Arche in France and the forty years since L'Arche began in the UK, in Kent. It turned out that Carlos had been listening to the CD in the car on the way over (as he often did, apparently: I think he was my number one fan!). I gladly sang the song.

Other musicians offered pieces, and there was a range of instruments on offer so that everyone could join in. It was a great evening, much enjoyed by all, and I was glad I'd decided that year to do something for my birthday. It was a good and hopeful *and* musical start to the year.

P.S. The title of this chapter was inspired in part by a comment made almost twenty years before by a friend of mine, Christopher John. Chris, a New Zealander, is a member and currently Minister General of SSF, the Society of St Francis, a worldwide Anglican Franciscan congregation. He founded an SSF community in Korea, which is where I met him in 2000 when I was there with my family. I was teaching a couple of classes at the Anglican University in Seoul and Chris was also part of the English Department there. One of our jobs was to organise in the summer an 'English camp' for some of the students over at the beautiful East Sea. We didn't manage to get the students to speak a lot of English but we had a fantastic time with them, at the beach and in the karaoke bar. And it was on the way to the karaoke bar one evening that Chris uttered words that stayed with me: 'Well, you're only forty-four once!'

30. DANIEL O'LEARY RIP

I was sad to hear of the death in January 2019 of Daniel O'Leary, the well-known and clearly much-loved priest, spiritual writer and retreat-giver.

Daniel was a Kerryman who spent much of his priestly ministry in the Leeds diocese and also taught theology and religious studies at St Mary's, Strawberry Hill. His writings had a certain light touch, and indeed he had at one time a regular piece in the *Tablet* called 'Travelling Light'; yet what he had to say was profound, very down to earth, and had an evident authenticity. There are none of us on this earth who are without our struggles, and I'm sure that Daniel had his, but he was able to make something creative from it. His slim but inspiring volume, *The Happiness Habit*, contains, among many other gems, a piece of Hasidic wisdom: 'Rake the muck this way, rake the muck that way; it will still be muck. Instead, start dancing your life thankfully on this beautiful earth.'

The theme of thankfulness and gratitude is a common one in Daniel's writing. He encourages us in *The Healing Habit* to repeat at the beginning of every day the words 'Thank you', and he quotes Meister Eckhart, the thirteenth-century German mystic: 'If the words Thank You were the only ones you ever uttered, you would become a magnet for love and beauty.'

Reading some of the obituaries following Daniel's death, I was struck by a sense of humanity and compassion; of him being always prepared to meet and accept people where they were. Jonathan Tulloch recounted in the *Tablet* the joy of a neighbour when Daniel had agreed to baptise her granddaughter, when they had been refused by another priest. Tulloch was later brought by this neighbour to Mass at Daniel's parish of St Wilfrid's in Ripon. He found himself in a packed congregation amidst a troupe of Morris dancers who had been organised to accompany the offertory procession. I think I would have enjoyed a Daniel O'Leary Mass!

Another common theme in Daniel's writing is the call for us to get in touch with those parts of us wherein lie our deepest longings and dreams. *The Happiness Habit* begins with a quote from Howard Thurman: 'Don't ask what the world needs. Ask yourself what makes you come alive and then go and do that. Because what the world needs is people who have come alive.'

I give thanks for your life Daniel. You seem to have lived it well, and I am inspired by you to try and do likewise.

31. IN PRISON AND YOU CAME TO SEE ME

I was at Mass in Maynooth with the Irish Catholic bishops and the gospel reading from Matthew 25 for the first Monday in Lent was especially apt:

I was hungry and you gave me food
I was thirsty and you gave me drink
I was a stranger and you made me welcome
Naked, and you clothed me
Sick, and you visited me
In prison and you came to see me.

In my student days there were many long, and sometimes heated, discussions between members of the Catholic Society, of which I was President for a year, and the Christian Union about who could be 'saved'. Was faith alone sufficient or were 'good works' also necessary? The bishop who gave the sermon at the Mass was in no doubt that service to neighbour is central, in particular the neighbour who is most in need. And just like the people in that gospel passage that Jesus told the story to, we may never know when we have helped, or harmed, another person with our words or our deeds.

By a happy coincidence, whilst I was in Maynooth enjoying again the warm hospitality of the bishops, Breda, Ellena and Liz from the Irish Chaplaincy were at Parliament to receive the Gerry Ryan Community Award from the Labour Party Irish Society in recognition of the great work of ICPO, the

Irish Council for Prisoners Overseas. In a typical year, those from the London office, which is part of Irish Chaplaincy, visit about 800 Irish prisoners across England and Wales, as well as roughly 400 Travellers in the criminal justice system. ICPO Maynooth, meanwhile, helps Irish people in prison elsewhere in the world. In addition, there is a wide range of office-based support including letter writing, and some financial assistance for phone credit, which is essential when the family is back in Ireland, and basic necessities like toiletries. We hear time and again from prisoners and others how vital, and at times literally life-saving, this support is, and we receive many messages of thanks. A man in HMP Hull told our Fr Gerry: 'I want to thank you for being there for me all these years. Just to have a friendly someone to talk to makes all the difference.' Gerry would himself have been with the others at Parliament but he was away at the time visiting other prisons in the North of England.

'In prison and you came to see me.'

When going off to University as an eighteen-year-old I'd sought to deepen my faith, leading me to get involved with the Catholic Society, which had great parties as well as great Masses. And I'd also wanted to find some kind of practical expression for this faith. I initially joined Student Community Action but my first couple of visits with them didn't seem to go too well and I didn't go again. Then a man from Belfast called Adrian arrived at the Catholic Chaplaincy. He was doing post-graduate studies in Japanese of all things, and he promptly started a student SVP (St Vincent de Paul) group which organised various weekly visiting: to a cancer hospital and a geriatric hospital near the campus; besides running parties for the children of Travellers. I eventually got involved but my first SVP visit didn't go very well either, and I was worried I wasn't really cut out for 'that kind of thing'. One of my friends, Tim, encouraged me to persevere, which I did, and I came to particularly enjoy my time with the people in the geriatric hospital, and I always seemed to come away feeling that I'd surely received far more than I could have given.

Following my time at Maynooth I drove to Prosperous, also in Co. Kildare, to stay with the above-mentioned Adrian and his three lovely daughters. I was on the receiving end of further warm hospitality, made especially so by a roaring peat fire and (even if it was Lent and I was trying to stay off alcohol) a very drinkable bottle of Australian red!

At times, the identity of the person in need is clear; at other times it may not be so, and I've always been struck by the command given in Hebrews 13 (with reference to a story in Genesis 18 where Abraham and Sarah give food to three unexpected visitors): 'Remember always to welcome strangers, for by doing this, some have entertained angels without knowing it.' Interestingly this is followed by the line:

'Keep in mind those who are in prison, as though you were in prison with them; and those who are being badly treated, since you too are in the one body.'

I certainly do believe that we are all part of one body, and that those parts that may be considered of less worth are perhaps in need of the greatest care.

32. THE MOST AMAZING YELLOW

We were barely half-way into Lent 2019 and I was starting to think, 'What's the point of it?' and, 'Shouldn't I be feeling more spiritual and Lent-like?' (whatever that's supposed to feel like). And I'd already broken my Lenten alcohol fast three times!

No. 1 was International Women's Day. Yim Soon said that merited a bottle of wine, and who was I to argue! No. 2 was the visit to my friend Adrian when I was in Kildare, and whose very nice bottle of Australian red, drunk in front of a roaring peat fire, was mentioned in the last chapter. No. 3 was the Ethnic Chaplains' meal at the Italian Chaplaincy to mark the feast of St Joseph. The Italians always lay on a feast, and it would have been rude to refuse the constant refills of the wine glass! Yim Soon's birthday was coming up soon as well, so lapse No. 4 was on the cards. I could say, in my defence, that in ancient Irish culture; also, interestingly, amongst the very ascetic desert fathers and mothers of the third century onwards, a fast would always be broken in order to offer hospitality to a guest and to share food and drink with them i.e. not just to sit and watch the guest eat and drink, rather to eat and drink *with* them.

Maybe I was just feeling a little bit cranky, and ironically it was after a long weekend staying at a monastery so I thought I should have been feeling completely at peace and, well, 'Lent-like'! I was reminded of a comment made to me one time by a monk who I'd got to know quite well having visited his monastery many times over the years. He was speaking to me just after Easter and said, with a rather pained expression, 'By the end of Lent I wanted to start throwing things in the refectory!' Welcome to the human race brother!

So what *is* the point of Lent? We make such a big deal of it in the Church; there must be some point to it! Perhaps it's good to remember what we are remembering during this season. It's the story of Jesus going into a desert for a long period *and* being tempted, by things it's easy to be tempted by, e.g. power and prestige. I guess there are times when we just have to face our demons. But it's worth noting as well that deserts, as well as being bleak and inhospitable, can also contain great beauty if only we are able to see and hear.

I enjoy each year the daily Lenten reflections of Brian Draper; so too the comments, pictures, poems and songs, even Facebook links, from his worldwide community of readers. Brian encourages us to take a 'mid-day moment', i.e. a time to stop, be still, and to simply notice. I don't usually manage to do this at noon but try at other points in the day. One of the most special moments for me during my monastery stay had been hearing an owl hooting in the middle of the night, then looking out of the window and seeing a clear starry sky with Orion and the winter triangle directly above.

Once when leading a retreat in the springtime at Minster Abbey in Kent I suggested that the participants walk slowly and mindfully around the beautifully kept garden and to see the colour yellow as if for the first time. Recalling that, I'd been revelling in the forsythia in full bloom in my own garden and thinking, 'Wow, that's the most amazing it's ever looked,' and, 'It's the most yellow it's ever been,' and I suppose I think that every year! Likewise when I went out early in the morning one day to find a late frost and delighted in the incredible patterns it made on the cars I thought it was the most amazing frost I'd ever seen. And it's fitting perhaps that the word Lent comes from an old English word for Springtime. A little bit of penance probably can't do us too much harm. But rejoicing in the beauty and the new life springing up everywhere, and in the daily unexpected gifts that are presented to us, might do us a lot more good.

Eyes to see and ears to hear: this is a common theme both in the Old Testament and in the teachings of Jesus. What do we see during the season of Lent, as well as at other times, and what do we hear? And could it be the most amazing thing we've ever seen and the most amazing thing we've ever heard?

33. THE BEST MEDICINE

When coming away from my regular visit to one of our Irish Chaplaincy seniors I was reflecting on how uplifted I felt and how it had to do, in part, by how much we had laughed during the visit. This particular lady was only in her seventies, but had fairly advanced dementia, and her sister had moved over from Ireland to stay in the one-bedroom flat as a live-in carer. It was a challenging situation but we always regaled one another with funny stories, and how we hooted with laughter.

One of the books of James Martin, the American Jesuit, is called *Between Heaven and Mirth*, with the sub-title 'Why joy, humour and laughter are at the heart of the spiritual life'. He speaks of the importance of humour, especially in religious settings which can easily become terribly serious and joyless. I imagine, sadly, that there are many people who might consider laughter to be incompatible with church or religion. And I'd been interested to see in a recent survey in the Church of England that people didn't want their priests to be cracking lots of jokes in their sermons! It's true that humour doesn't really come across in the gospels. I fear this is a case of jokes getting lost in translation, besides the notion that religion is a 'serious business'. I like to think that the stories of Jesus were filled with humour and hilarity, and that he liked nothing better than to have a good laugh with some of the dodgy characters he hung out with.

I still remember the words of my dear friend Tony (and the jokes he told) in his best man speech at my wedding. He reminded us that the words 'humour', 'humility' and 'human' all come from the Latin word 'humus' which means earth or ground, so that when we laugh we are connected in a particular way with the ground we walk upon and with those we walk with. It could be said indeed that a sure sign of a growing connection and intimacy with another person is the ability to laugh together. Physiologically, as well, it's healthy for us to laugh. A good, hearty laugh can relieve physical tension and stress and leave the muscles relaxed for up to forty-five minutes. It boosts the immune system, decreases stress hormones and increases immune cells and infection-fighting antibodies, therefore improving resistance to disease. It also reduces blood pressure and releases endorphins, the body's natural painkillers. Laughter is almost as good for the body as going to the gym! And it doesn't cost a penny in membership! I remember at one time somebody in the NHS having the idea of sending comedians into hospitals to help patients to laugh but sadly it didn't seem to catch on.

And talking of funny people, I was tickled to hear what happened when John Cleese met the Dalai Lama. They didn't say a word to one another but simply broke into spontaneous and prolonged laughter! James Martin tells us in his book that the Trappist monk and prolific spiritual writer Thomas Merton could be identified by visitors to his monastery in Kentucky (at a time, in the 1960s, when there were 200 monks there) because he was the one who was always laughing. And one of the many nice stories in the book concerns Mother Teresa from the time when John Paul II was pope and creating loads of new saints. A young sister asked what she would have to do in her life to achieve sainthood. Mother Teresa replied, 'Die now; this pope's canonising everyone!'

The season of Lent is perhaps not readily associated with fun and frivolity. Yet, in the scripture readings from Ash Wednesday at the beginning of Lent we have in Matthew 6 Jesus warning us not to look miserable when we fast; and we are reminded of the words from Isaiah 58 of the kind of fast that is pleasing to God:

LOOKING AHEAD WITH HOPE

To let the oppressed go free,
And break every yoke,
To share your bread with the hungry,
And shelter the homeless poor.

And, I would add, try and have a bit of a laugh with people as well. It's one of the things that binds us most profoundly together in our common humanity; and it really is a great medicine.

34. A SMALL AND WONDERFUL WORLD

My friend Richard and I first met when we were part of the group of new assistants at L'Arche Kent at the end of the 1980s, a group which included Yim Soon. Richard was a member of the music group at our wedding, which also had in it Lucy Winkett of St James's, Piccadilly.

Richard, in his post-L'Arche life, is a senior social worker in the field of mental health and he lives in Lewes in Sussex with Susan and their two gorgeous little girls. We don't get to see each other too often, but when we do we have a great time: re-telling some of the stories from our treasure trove of shared history and interesting characters; and catching up on the latest news. I'd barely seen him since starting at the Irish Chaplaincy so there was a lot to tell: both about how I came to be part of such a special organisation and about some of the adventures I'd had.

We were in a newly-opened bar in Lewes, a bit off the beaten track, and Richard was just off to get the second round of beer. Yes, I'm afraid it was yet another lapse from my Lenten alcohol fast, but hey, we hadn't seen each other for a long time. I looked around the pub and, to my surprise, saw a familiar face. A few days previously, on my way to work, I had bumped into Anton, the Belfast-born actor who lives in Camden and who performed at our concert in St James's at the end of January. He had told me how, the night before, somebody had said to him how much she had enjoyed the concert and hoped we would do it again. I assured Anton that we were indeed planning another and that he would be on the bill.

Well there I was in a back-street bar in deepest Sussex

and there was Anton! He was as taken aback as I was, and he recalled to Richard his role in a play that I'd commissioned from London-based 'Irish Theatre'. It was called *Irish Chaplaincy- 60 Years On*, and Anton told how the performance in Wormwood Scrubs prison had been the most amazing experience of his professional life; and he explained how he and I had bumped into each other the other day and about the person who had asked about the concert. And this, on an evening when I had been telling my friend about some of what I would call the 'grace-filled' circumstances that had led me to the Irish Chaplaincy and into subsequent situations. Richard and I were both agreed that some of the things that happen to us in our lives, and some of the encounters that take place at particular times, can surely not be explained away as mere 'coincidence'.

Back at the house later on, the guitars came out and Susan produced her violin and we had a good session till the early hours which included an old favourite of ours, 'Over You' by The Undertones. I went on to sing The Fureys' classic 'When you were sweet 16', which I'd especially enjoyed singing the previous day at a care home in West London where I'd been going once a month to perform Irish songs. Richard was clearly touched by the song, as was Susan, and he explained to me that his mum and a brother of hers, a Servite priest who I'd actually met thirty years before and who had introduced Richard to L'Arche, used to sing it when he was a child. And I found out for the first time that Richard's mum not only had been born in Northern Ireland, her family having moved to England when she was in her early teens, but not far from my own mum, in Co. Down. That song also happens to be Yim Soon's favourite.

I'm struck more and more by how inter-connected we are; by how our stories weave in and out of one another's; and by this mysterious action of grace which appears to be at work in and around us and which binds and re-binds us together in the most incredible and joyful and healing ways.

It is a small world, and a very wonderful one.

35. THE FISHERMAN'S TRAIL

A highlight of my walking week in Portugal was having a beer with a group of ten Spanish people and singing Irish songs with them on request.

I was there with Yim Soon to walk for five days on what is known in English as the Fisherman's Trail, a series of paths that follow the rugged and beautiful Atlantic coastline along cliff-tops and beaches, so-called because they were used by the fishermen to gain access to remote bays and coves. We had bumped into the Spanish group on our first evening. They were sitting outside a bar in the town square as we got off the bus from Lisbon and I asked if they knew where our hotel was. One of them began to speak in good English and kindly offered to take us there.

Yim Soon was unable to walk for the first three days, having injured her ankles whilst training for the long hikes, so I walked the 15-25 km per day while she took a taxi to the next place. I was usually glad of company and on the third day I came across the Spaniards on the trail and we got chatting. They were all teachers from the Basque country, three of them English teachers, and Anna, it turned out, was married to Noel who's originally from Dublin and whose mother is from Galway. I told her that my dad had been a Galwayman and that was it; I was instantly accepted into their group. I complimented Luis, the man who'd shown us where to go on the first evening, on his English and he said he'd learnt it from Noel, to whom he goes twice a week for conversation. Luis hadn't quite mastered the Dublin accent but he knew one or two choice expressions; and I taught him one or two more to take back to his next lesson with Noel!

We spoke a lot about Dublin and I was impressed (because it's one of my favourite films) that Anna was friends with Brian Mac Aodha who plays the pipes in a scene in *The Commitments*. She'd met Brian's brother on her first trip to Dublin as an eighteen-year-old au pair, a trip on which she'd also met her husband-to-be. I thought, 'Here I am walking along a cliff in Portugal with a group of Spanish people, one of whom has a mother-in-law from Galway and who knows someone who appeared in *The Commitments*: how wonderful!'

It got even better. The group told me how they had a little routine on their frequent walking trips. At the end of the day's hike the first thing they do is find a bar and have a beer. I really hoped they would invite me to join them for a beer. And they did! And as we sat outside a bar in their destination village drinking our beer, Anna asked if I knew 'The Wild Rover'. Well, who doesn't know 'The Wild Rover'! I duly sang it, and then gladly sang it a second time, recorded 'for Noel'! I sang a few more songs and Luis and a couple of the others added some nice harmonies. And I did 'The Galway Shawl' for my dad and for Anna's mother-in-law. Then they sang a couple of songs in Spanish, and there was even one in Basque. It was utterly magical.

I had to walk on a few extra kilometres to where Yim Soon and I were staying that night so didn't see the Spaniards the following day, but at the end of the fifth and final day's hiking when we were sitting in a village square having a drink with Steen and Anni from Denmark whom we'd got to know along the route (no Irish connection there but they were lovely all the same!) the group suddenly appeared, coming for their customary beer, and we greeted one another like long-lost friends.

I thought of that phrase I'd learnt from a man I met 'by chance' on the Camino in Spain, when telling him I'd spoken the previous day with a Spaniard who was married to a woman from Newry who knew my Uncle Pat: '*El mundo es un pañuelo*', the world is a handkerchief. And what an amazing and richly woven handkerchief it is.

36. EVERYONE'S A WINNER?

We are blessed at the Irish Chaplaincy with a lot of fantastic volunteers and it was not easy to have to choose just one of them to nominate for the Irish in Britain Volunteer Awards. We did in the end nominate somebody and I was saying to Paul, 'If that person gets the award it's good for everyone at the Chaplaincy', and I added, 'Everyone's a winner.' I thought for a few moments, then said, 'But not in the Champions League final!'

It was the day before the big match and Paul, who is from Liverpool, was going to be cheering for the reds, whereas Rory, who works with Paul in the Seniors' Project, is a big Spurs fan! Even though I was a relative neutral I was also excited about the game and I have fond memories of the 2005 Champions League final in which Liverpool were up against AC Milan. I was in Assisi at the time, attending an international L'Arche meeting, and I went off to a bar in the evening with people from L'Arche Liverpool and an assortment of football fans from various countries. It looked like it was all over by half-time, with Milan, the favourites, having raced into a 3-0 lead, so I went off to join a prayer vigil in the nearby Cathedral, which was the official item on the programme for the L'Arche gathering! When I got back to the bar I was informed that an on-fire Steven Gerrard had just pulled one back with a towering header and I was just in time to see a perfect strike from Vladimir Smicer to make it 3-2. Then straight after that, Liverpool were awarded a penalty which Xabi Alonso put in on the rebound: 3-3! It all happened within six minutes. If I'd stayed praying any longer I would have missed it all! Liverpool won in the end on penalties and the bar erupted in celebration. Even the locals were rooting for Liverpool as the favoured team in Assisi is AS Roma, fierce rivals of Milan. It was a special evening.

Another famous Liverpool comeback, this time against the mighty Barcelona, had brought them to the 2019 final. Tottenham too had come back from the dead in their semi-final against Ajax, so there was great excitement in the English press about an all-English final, with stories of people paying up to £25,000 for a top-priced ticket. There was a piece in the *Evening Standard* about four Spurs fans who were offered £15,000 for their four £60 tickets. They turned it down. And to the question 'Will it be worth it?' the answer was, 'We'll let you know on Sunday', i.e. the day after the match.

By all accounts there was a great atmosphere in Madrid, the venue for the final, which was besieged by tens of thousands of fans wearing either white or red and singing their respective anthems. It strikes me that football provides for people some of the elements that organised religion once gave the majority: for example, coming together in a grand venue for worship and singing. Many of the football chants even use the tunes of old hymns, like the favourite of the Tottenham fans, 'When the Spurs go marching in'. And communal singing is good for our health, releasing endorphins (the 'happy hormone') and oxytocin (the 'love hormone'), which can reduce anxiety and stress. Having said that, watching football is hardly a relaxing past-time!

It wasn't a great game in the end (finals rarely are) but I enjoyed watching it with a few old mates from my football-playing days, and we reminisced about some of our triumphs on the pitch, whilst conveniently forgetting about the disappointments! There had to be a winner on the night and it was the team in red, so the song that rang out in the stadium at the end was the most famous football anthem of all, 'You'll never walk alone'. I was reflecting on how the Spurs fans must have been feeling, probably pretty gutted, but I hoped they wouldn't think that they'd made a wasted trip, and that they really should have taken the thousands of pounds on offer for their tickets, but could appreciate being part of a really special occasion, even if not all could be on the winning side.

One of the most enjoyable football matches I ever played in was one I organised in Canterbury between L'Arche Kent and L'Arche Bognor. On both teams there were people with and without learning disabilities, men and women, young and old. There were people kicking the ball towards the 'wrong' goal. And when somebody scored everybody cheered. It was such fun and truly everyone was a winner that day. Ironically it was at the venue where I played a lot of competitive matches, when every game seemed like a matter of life or death. And I'll add here the famous quote of the legendary Liverpool manager Bill Shankly: 'Football is not a matter of life or death … it's much more important than that!'

It can be good, I think, for us to work hard and to use our talents to achieve great things, in the world of sport or elsewhere, and it certainly feels good to be on the winning side. But failure and disappointment are also part of life, and they can be a spur for us to try even harder next time to realise our dreams. And whoever was to be chosen as Irish in Britain's Volunteer of the Year I hoped we'd all be able to rejoice with them and with their organisation and declare that, in some aspects of life at least, everyone's a winner.

As it turned out, the Irish in Britain volunteer of the year for 2019 was our very own Sr Moira, in recognition of her many years of working with Irish prisoners. Moira, originally from Galway, was one of those people I'd met at the Chaplaincy when I went for my interview and who I'd felt so at home with. We were all delighted, especially Moira.

37. I WOULD WALK 500 MILES

I was worried that I was getting a bit fed up with singing '500 Miles' every year in an Alpine cave.

There I was, back for the eighth time in the French Alps with a wonderful and very international group of seventy-five people from L'Arche. It's the week-long event called the 'Walking Retreat' and the cave is where we always go on the Wednesday. We're well warmed up by that point, with a 'tester' hike of a few kilometres on the Monday, followed on the Tuesday by a proper mountain, La Scia, whose summit is just under 2000m. Getting to the top, besides a lot of walking up-hill, includes going along a narrow trail which is very close to a cliff edge. I don't think it would be allowed in the UK with Health & Safety being what it is: nor the climb into the cave on the Wednesday, involving as it does a final scramble up an almost vertical bit of rock face right next to a waterfall whilst clinging onto a rope. In the more than twenty years that the retreat has been going nobody has been lost yet! One of the women in my small group was pretty scared when she saw the route up to the cave but so proud when she made it in.

I was one of the last into the cave and the music was already in full swing, with my musical partner Emmanuel knocking out some French songs on his guitar which some of the younger guys had kindly carried up the mountain (rather them than me). We also had with us that year a lovely young German woman Annika, who had brought her ukulele. The crowd wanted '500 Miles', and who was I to disappoint them.

I'd done it the previous two years in the cave, as well as at other times in the week, and it had been a quite magical experience. This time it was very good but the fact that it wasn't absolutely amazing made it feel like a let-down. 'Maybe I've just done this too many times,' I said to myself, a little sadly, 'the song, the cave, the Alps retreat.' And I wondered if it was time to call it a day.

I had an interesting dream that night. I owed one of the young men €20 for drinks. In reality, the guys had been treating me to a beer each day following our freezing but exhilarating post-walk dip in a mountain river. In the dream I gave him a €50 note in expectation of him giving me €30 in change. He gave me two notes which I thought must be a €20 and a €10 but when I looked more closely I saw that he'd given me a €20 note and a €50 note. The message of the dream seemed to be that I'd given quite a lot but had been given back even more. I shared the dream at breakfast with Islay, with whom I'd had some lovely conversations and who had been telling me about her dreams during the retreat. I also told her about my slightly complicated feelings at the cave. She suggested that I just had to sing something different next year! But then later that day David who used to lead the organising team said to me with his face glowing, '500 Miles: that song is at the heart of the retreat for me.' And I thought to myself, 'Hey, singing that song every year in a cave at the top of a waterfall in the French Alps with a fantastic bunch of people and sharing a joyful moment with them: it's not really a terrible hardship, is it!'

Music is an important element of the retreat and there are certain 'hit songs' each year from the booklet and which get stuck into people's heads which is kind of nice to see. And I was touched to receive an email from Islay a year later telling me about a walking holiday she'd just made with another Alps veteran and how they'd been singing some of the songs from the retreat. On the Friday morning of the 2019 gathering, after the final talk and before the last walk, there was time for one more song. Emmanuel and I thought a few moments. Which of the great songs we'd done that week were we going to go out walking to? Yes, of course: '500 Miles'. I toned it down a little and it worked just fine and everyone loved it and so did I.

We leave on the Saturday morning and a lot of the group get a bus down to Grenoble to catch trains or buses onwards. Annika got out her ukulele and everyone sang and it was so uplifting and she even did a good ukulele version of '500 Miles'. I'll suggest that to The Proclaimers next time I see them! They must get a bit fed up as well sometimes with singing it. On arrival at the station we went into the waiting-room and got out the instruments and started to sing. It was such a lovely way to end the retreat, an outpouring and sharing of sheer joy. Lots of people who passed by began to smile and to give the thumbs up. Several took videos on their phones. A message came through later from some of those who'd caught a bus from Grenoble to say that there was a man on the bus who was listening to a video of us singing at the station! And David informed me later on the train to Paris that videos had been posted on the station Facebook page. As we were launching into '500 Miles' an office door opened and a member of the station staff asked if we could just turn it down a little! No problem: it was slightly less exuberant, but no less wonderful because of that.

The Alps retreat is an experience of having the heart filled to overflowing with sheer goodness. And I suppose I'll be back again for No. 9, as long as I'm invited, and as soon as such events are allowed to take place again (like everything else, it was cancelled in 2020). And I'm sure I'll be singing again, even in the cave:

And I would walk 500 Miles, and I would walk 500 more
Just to be the man who walks a thousand miles to fall down
at your door.

109

38. HOW TO LIVE SEVEN YEARS LONGER

Research has shown some interesting health benefits enjoyed by people who practise gratitude.

Apparently if just before going to bed I recall three of the most beautiful moments of the day and savour and give thanks for them then I will sleep better and more deeply. Practising gratitude has also been shown to lessen feelings of stress, anxiety, despair and depression; and to lead to feelings of joy, love, satisfaction with life, and to improved mental health. It is said to give energy and increase motivation; it helps us achieve our objectives; and it gives meaning to life, confidence in the future, and an enhanced love of self. Improved relationships and better communication are also said to occur. Gratitude can help couples get on better and stay together longer. And in the workplace it contributes to a better atmosphere, it nourishes the links between people, and it augments the motivation and efficiency of the team. It helps one make friends, feel more included, and to be more appreciated by others.

There are financial benefits, with daily practice of meditation being said to lessen the need for compulsive spending or eating with which we may try to fill an inner emptiness. I was especially surprised to hear that gratitude can even slow down the ageing process, and this was demonstrated by a study of a community of nuns in Minnesota. The nuns each wrote a letter when they entered the convent and further letters at the ages of forty and seventy. The letters were later examined with reference to vocabulary related to gratitude and it was found that those who had lived in a spirit of gratitude lived on average seven years longer than those who did not.

Gratitude has been shown to lead to altruistic behaviour. In a restaurant in Philadelphia in 2009 two customers went to the till to pay and were told that someone had already paid their bill. They responded by paying the bill of the next customers. This continued for five hours, with each customer paying the bill of the following customer, and giving generous tips besides. Kindness begets kindness.

And a remarkable thing happened in Los Angeles in 1995. I know because I was there, together with Yim Soon and our then eight-month-old son Kieran. We'd been at an event in Portland, Oregon during which I'd had my guitar stolen. After the event we'd gone to LA to spend three days with a friend of Yim Soon but she'd lost the address. So there we were in this huge city with our luggage, a young child and an empty guitar case; and with nowhere to stay and not much money left. We managed to make contact with a Korean priest we'd known in Canterbury. He arranged for us to be picked up by two Korean nuns who took us to their convent in the Koreatown and fed us and gave us a large, air-conditioned room for the night. For the next two days and nights we were welcomed by members of the Korean Catholic community. One of those we met, after enquiring as to how I came to have an empty guitar case, said to me, 'I want you to have my guitar.' The guitar I was given that day is no ordinary guitar: it's a hand-made Ovation. And it's no ordinary Ovation either: it has an intricate design and a lovely, resonant tone. Ironically, or rather fittingly, the personal theme for me on that event in Portland had been gratitude.

That guitar has served me well over the years, and I've always felt relatively relaxed about sharing it with others. It had been a particular joy for me to bring the guitar into Wormwood Scrubs prison to sing Irish songs to a group of

Travellers, and to then have it played by a guy who had been a sessions musician. That guitar was given to me as a gift, and gifts are to be shared.

And so whether or not we want to live seven years longer, or simply get a better night's sleep, all we need to do is say thank you!

39. THOUGHTS FROM MY CELL

I awoke in my cell having had an interesting dream in which I was in a kind of social club with my guitar (the one mentioned in the last chapter) playing 'Country Roads' with lots of people singing along.

It's one of the songs I'd sung at a prison event a couple of days before, after one of the men said he liked American Country songs and sang a couple himself. He had a really good voice and wasn't at all shy. None of the others, though, seemed too interested in singing and were happy to sit and chat with one another and with those of us from the Irish Chaplaincy, away from their cells for a blessed couple of hours.

I should explain that the cell I was in was at the monastery where I go regularly to spend twenty-four hours in silence, and I was particularly curious on that occasion as to why the monastic tradition gives the same name to the bedroom of the monk as that used in prisons for the place of confinement. It was an interesting link to our Traveller event at Wormwood Scrubs, so too the dream.

Our event at the Scrubs had been surprisingly relaxed, especially considering that it was one of the hottest days of the year, when the tiny, airless cells must be like infernos. We were in the multi-faith room, with doors wide open (exceptionally) and fans whirring, and the space was laid out café style, with tables and easy chairs. There was a lot of pleasant conversation, a little bit of singing (not too much, and that was fine). And then there was the food: a feast of bacon and cabbage and potatoes, with lots left over for the guys to take back to their mates who hadn't been able to attend, or to eat again themselves in their cells. And after the meal there were more treats like chocolate that Breda and Ellena had brought. Several of the prison staff came along. Sarah the governor was there, with several of her senior staff, plus Zahid the head of Chaplaincy and Fr Chima the RC chaplain. They also enjoy and value our events, and it's probably a bit of light relief for them from the major challenges involved in running a prison. Years of under-investment and over-crowding have taken their toll; and when availability to drugs is thrown into the mix and prisoners locked up for large parts of the day then there are some highly dangerous and volatile situations created.

Following the food there was a group photo outside with everybody in great spirits, and then there was time to help people with a questionnaire about our 'Travelling Forward Resettlement Project'. I was struck that in answer to the question about previous education most of the guys ticked '1' (the lowest score), whilst for the questions about interest in training and in being helped to get a post-release job most ticked '5' (the highest). And the majority of the men needed somebody to write down their replies for them.

I don't know what these men have done to end up in prison, and I don't need to know. I simply enjoy the time with them: sharing a nice meal together and having a bit of craic. And they're so appreciative of these events. For Travellers, who are used to moving around and being out of doors, being confined to a small cell for prolonged periods must be a particular hardship.

As time was called on the gathering, the two hours having flown by, there were multiple handshakes and 'Thank you' was said repeatedly. And then it was back to the cell. In my monastic cell, from which I could hear the gentle sound of rain through the open window and look out at the woods surrounding the monastery, and from which I could leave whenever I wished, I thought of those guys.

40. I STILL AIN'T GOT NO BARMOUTH BLUES

There were two impressive cycling achievements at the Barmouth gathering in 2019: one of the group travelling there by bike from near Liverpool (Paul Devlin: 91 miles); and somebody (me!) making a successful ascent of what had been officially declared that year as the steepest road in the world.

Paul had made his epic journey with a friend, Ged Edwards, who, it turned out, had several connections with our group, which was celebrating its twentieth anniversary of getting together for the first week in August at the Jesuit House in North Wales in its stunning location overlooking Cardigan Bay. Ged works for CAFOD and had just been seconded to CSAN (Caritas Social Action Network), of which Irish Chaplaincy is a member, so he and I knew a few people in common. That included Sean Ryan of Caritas Salford (mentioned in previous chapters) who is the national lead for the Community Sponsorship Scheme. It was through leading this scheme in their local parish in Rainhill that Paul and Ged had become friends, and they had received valuable help from Sean in their hard work, over years and involving many people, to welcome a Syrian refugee family. The family had come at the end of July, mum and dad and three boys, and they were all smiling radiantly in the photos of their arrival at Manchester airport that were posted on our 'Barmouth Blues' WhatsApp group, having finally been able to leave a refugee camp for a new life.

We were getting a little concerned on the first day of the holiday when Paul and Ged, who'd been on their bikes since

7 a.m., hadn't appeared by 9.45 p.m., and with darkness having descended. It transpired that they'd reached the house an hour earlier but finding that they'd 'only' done 91 miles kept going up the road towards Harlech and back, to find they'd got to 99 miles, so did a little lap of Barmouth sea-front to clock up the magical ton. Perhaps you need to be somebody who indulges in extreme sports to fully appreciate why, after spending twelve hours in the saddle with your body screaming with pain, and having reached your destination, you would choose to keep going for a further hour! I would have done exactly the same in that situation!

Speaking of Harlech, that was the scene for my own bit of extreme sport, namely attempting to cycle up a road towards the castle with an average gradient of 22 per cent, according to the book 'Britain's Steepest Cycling Climbs', and reaching almost 40 per cent in places. I'd done a bit of training for it the week before, although there's nothing around Canterbury (or anywhere in the world for that matter!) that comes close to that level of steepness. And the previous day I'd done a recce by cycling *down* the street in question (scary even when going slowly!). On the day of the attempt I had a support team in the form of Paul Crilley who was waiting for me halfway up the hill to warn of any cars coming down. An added challenge is having to go the wrong way up a one-way street! I was in luck. The road had just been closed to traffic for the day for a pipe replacement and I thought, 'It's now or never.' I said a couple of Hail Marys and went for it. I made it up the first and steepest section, which looks almost vertical when you see it from the bottom, and just kept going. Three people walking (very slowly!) up the hill cheered me on, so too the workmen further up and when I reached the top I felt *so* pleased with myself.

It was one of the highlights for me of Barmouth 2019. Another was, as it usually is, the early morning runs on the beach followed by a dip in the sea, which was not *quite* as cold as it had been in past years. The concert night is also great fun. Young and old take a turn and it was lovely to have some absent friends in Ireland with us via some kind of amazing modern technology and even singing with us, albeit with a slight time lag! A staple of the evening is still '500 Miles' performed (particularly well that year, I thought) by Tony and me; so too the men's obligatory rendition of Chris de Burgh's 'Patricia the Stripper'.

The week flies by and then it's time to pack and to clean the house and go our separate ways. It's back to work or uni. or school or wherever. Life goes on. But how lovely it is to have a chance, at least for a week, to be with old friends in a beautiful place, eating well (a different family producing a feast every evening), having fun, and doing a bit of extreme sport besides. We were already counting the days till the next Barmouth …

41. NEWRY GIRL TURNS NINETY

My mum was one of three ladies reaching the grand age of ninety at the care home in Coventry where she'd been living for the last year, and the home had organised a special celebration which included a versatile entertainer.

Mr Gallagher, as he's known when he performs, was dressed in a very eye-catching yellow suit (for his St Patrick's Day appearance he'd had a green suit, and he explained to me later that he also dresses up as Elvis on demand). The dining room was decked out in disco lights and Mr Gallagher had added balloons and a placard with the names of the birthday girls: Gladys, Valerie and Alicia. Before starting to sing, he read out a little history of the lives of the three women. When he explained that Gladys had left school at fourteen to work in a mill she called out, 'No, I was thirteen!' It was very sensitively done, so too when he told some of mum's story: how she'd been born in Newry, Co Down, the second of ten surviving children of Elizabeth and Joseph McStay. Her favourite subject at school had been maths, but she'd had to leave at fourteen to work in Bessbrook Mill. She'd come to England in 1957 to take up a job in the café of Coventry railway station; had met her husband-to-be, a Galwayman, three months later at an Irish dance; and had married in 1960 and had two children, my sister Eileen and me. As mentioned earlier, mum had arrived in Coventry in probably the very month in 1957, September, that the Irish Chaplaincy was founded, in response to the thousands of people like my parents who had left Ireland in search of work.

The singing finally began, with Mr Gallagher going through the likes of 'When you're smiling', and 'We'll meet again', after which Gladys called out, 'You sing it ten times better than Vera Lynn!' He added a couple of Irish songs, 'The Rose of Tralee' and 'Your Lovely Irish Eyes'; and then he was into his Elvis repertoire, at which he particularly excelled.

After the entertainment there was the cutting of the cake and then food. Mum hadn't wanted to make a fuss of her nintieth birthday, but she enjoyed it. She was tired, though, by the end when we said goodbye in her room. I'm grateful that she can see out her final years in such a nice place with such kind staff. I'm grateful for the joyful and thoughtful celebration to mark her nintieth. And above all I'm grateful for this wonderful woman who brought me into the world and who has loved and cherished me.

42. A WEEK AT NODDFA

My eldest son Kieran was a bit mystified when I told him I was going on silent retreat for a week. 'What are you going to do?' he asked. 'Good question,' I replied. And my youngest son Sean was surprised when I called him a day into the retreat. 'I thought you weren't allowed to speak!' he said. 'It's your birthday,' I explained.

I had come to Noddfa, a big old house in a stunning location on the North Wales coast and whose name in Welsh means place of rest or refuge. To the front of the house are views over the beautiful Conwy Bay and to the back are the steep and rugged hills of Snowdonia which rise rapidly to 1,000 feet in height. Following my birthday greetings to Sean I switched off the phone and gradually sank into the silence. With reference to Kieran's question, one of the things I did was to walk a lot: up in the hills, and along by the sea. I even swam in the sea the first couple of days when the weather was still warm. It was pretty fresh at the end of September!

When, a year later, I was giving the opening talk on our Irish Chaplaincy Retreat via zoom I used the image of going into the mountains for being on retreat and mentioned my frequent forays into the hills at the back of Noddfa. I pointed out that throughout the Bible interesting things seem to happen on mountains; whether that's Moses being presented with the ten commandments or Jesus being transfigured. I explained as well that from the top of a mountain or high hill we have the chance to see things we wouldn't normally see, or to see them in a different way. I suggested that a retreat was an opportunity to see differently. It was nice to get an email that day from one of the group who recognised that the place I'd spoken about was Noddfa.

Besides all the walking I also took the time on retreat to just sit, whether on a bench in the garden or down at the seafront café with a cup of tea and a slice of bara brith (Welsh fruit cake). It was a week of living quite simply and slowly. I noticed as the days went by that my breathing had become slower and deeper. Even my walking slowed down. I wasn't in such a hurry, and I was becoming a bit more mindful of what there was around me: the touch of a leaf, the sight of a squirrel eating a nut, the shiny feel of a conker, walking barefoot in the lush green grass, the gentle sound of rain in the trees, or on my face as I was out for a stroll (it was Wales; there was quite a lot of rain!). Eating becomes more of a sensory experience when on retreat. I enjoyed looking at the colours and textures of the food, the touch of certain things, and the careful chewing and an increased awareness of the taste. Halfway through the week during breakfast I suddenly noticed the pictures on the cereal bowl. Those pictures on the bowls must have been there to start with but I just hadn't really seen them. So I suppose what I did during that week was begin to notice, to be aware, to be a little more mindful than usual of the world around me, of what I was eating, seeing, listening to; also of what was happening within me. There were the ups and downs that take place in any week, but there was the opportunity on retreat to be a bit more conscious about this.

It was a deeply creative week for me. I hadn't written a song for nearly two years but had brought a guitar, just in case 'something happened'. Well, goodness me did something happen! My retreat guide Lynne, who I spoke to each day, encouraged me to write a song and I ended up writing four. I sang three of them at the Masses which took place each afternoon for the group of about ten retreatants, and one woman said to me afterwards, 'That song really struck a chord.' I was touched as the week went on how, away from the usual 'distractions' of daily life, I was becoming not just more attuned to certain deeper 'movements' (for want of a better word) within myself but also in the group. Halfway through the retreat I'd been thinking to myself that, although it was pleasant to be there, walking in the hills and eating nice food, nothing really 'spectacular' was happening but then found a book in the library about dreams and had gone to bed having read about Carl Jung's theory of the collective unconscious. I woke the next morning having had a dream which not only featured a man playing on the guitar an old song but in a brilliant new way but also seemed to contain a reference to the collective unconscious. I thought, 'Yes, something quite interesting does seem to be happening here!' For the last couple of days of the retreat I was increasingly aware of a whole range of remarkable connections and of threads coming together.

Returning from retreat is never easy, and when back into the usual hubbub of life there's the question, 'Did that really happen?' One of the Bible stories I prayed with during the week was that story of the transfiguration in Matthew 17. Jesus had taken some of the apostles with him up a high mountain and had been transfigured and joined by Moses and Elijah. Peter remarks, 'It is wonderful for us to be here,' and he offers to build tents there on the mountain top. This suggests to me the desire to remain in this place of peak experience. However, just as Peter and the others had to come back down the mountain, so too must we return from retreat or holiday or whatever. Life goes on. But I assure myself that what happened in that week at Noddfa really did happen, and it really was wonderful to be there.

43. ALPINE ADVENTURES

My old friend Pat had invited me to spend a weekend with the assistants of L'Arche Grenoble with the instructions, 'Bring your guitar and your wife!' I happily obliged on both counts.

When Pat made his first trip to France as an eighteen-year-old, he didn't speak a word of French; his motivation being to learn enough to get him through the language part of his Leaving Cert. back in his native Cork. Now after living in in the country for over thirty-five years people think he's French. He's currently leader of L'Arche Grenoble, although he and his family still live in the old farmhouse, complete with donated swimming pool, near his previous L'Arche community La Vallée, where I'd spent a couple of weeks in 2012.

Yim Soon and I, and the guitar, duly arrived in the South of France and stayed the first night in the L'Arche house where I'd given a little impromptu concert the year before. There was a large gathering of people on that first evening, with lots of delicious cheese on offer, and I was pleased to see some familiar faces. I was touched when one woman said that she remembered me playing guitar at an event in France that I'd helped organise eight years previously. After a good night's sleep in the wooden-ceilinged house that the architect had designed to resemble a ski lodge, and with fantastic views of the mountains that surround Grenoble, we departed with a group of about thirty assistants to Chamrousse, a ski resort at an altitude of 1,700m (that's 5,800 ft: nearly twice the height of Snowdon!). I could feel that the air was a bit thinner than I'm used to and when we hiked up a rocky piste to a height of over 2,000m, and with a wind that was so strong it was almost blowing us off the mountain, I remarked to Pat that it didn't make me want to climb Everest! And we weren't even at a quarter of the height of the tallest mountain.

The highlight of the weekend was a musical session on the Saturday night. That was one of the main reasons, I think, that Pat had enlisted my services: he and I having shared some mighty sessions over the years. You never really know, when doing the first one or two songs, how well a session is going to take off. This one was still going strong at 1.30 a.m. and we'd worked our way through a very international and very eclectic mix of numbers. A young German woman also had a guitar and sang an Amy Winehouse song just like Amy Winehouse. She followed that up with some of her own songs in German which were simply beautiful. Then a young woman from Vietnam announced, 'I like Christmas songs,' so I launched into 'Fairytale of New York' and that led somehow to George Michael's 'Last Christmas', which must have been a big hit in France because everyone was belting out the words with gusto. When Pat produced a large bottle of Chartreuse, the strong green liqueur produced by the Carthusian monks in their monastery nearby and which I associate with my times in the Alps, it was the cherry on the icing on the cake.

At the end of the weekend, Pat drove Yim Soon and I to a massif on the other side of Grenoble, to the village of St Pierre de Chartreuse where the Alps retreat takes place each June. We had rented a studio apartment (i.e. bedsit!) for five nights and I planned to show Yim Soon some of the walks that we do on the retreat. I was bitterly disappointed to arrive there and find that the studio was tiny, having been sure it had looked quite big in the picture on the internet! The weather wasn't great either, with almost non-stop rain for the first two days, so that some of the walks could have been too dangerous in the wet and slippery conditions. There were a few books in the apartment, one of which was *The Art of Happiness* by the Dalai Lama. I read a bit of it and I think it helped me to view the situation in a different way i.e. to try to accept, be content with and be thankful for whatever is given, rather than being disappointed that it's not something else. I decided that the studio was plenty big enough for us. Besides, it had a nice little balcony from which I could see (when it wasn't raining or misty!) the impressive Chamechaude, the highest peak in the Chartreuse mountain range and which resembles the mountain at the start of Paramount films! And even in the rain we did some nice walks, although I must admit that it was a welcome treat when the weather cleared on the third day and the sun appeared and I could take in the incredible scenery around us.

We managed to hike up La Scia which has a peak of 1,800m, having started at 900m down in the village. That was my favourite walk of the week and it was rounded off in a special way by an encounter on the way down with a man called Jean-Pierre and his lovely six-year-old daughter Rose. They were from Lyon and were spending two weeks in the area, being joined for the second week by his wife and their baby son. 'Is there much to do here for children?' I asked, having been struck by how few people there were outside of the summer or the ski season. 'Not really,' he replied, 'but it's nice to be out in the nature, and to pick mushrooms.' And Rose looked so content to be out walking with her dad. Jean-Pierre showed me the bag of mushrooms they'd picked and Rose proudly announced that she'd found two of them (her dad later explained to me that those two were probably poisonous!). Back in the village we had drinks at the bakery and Yim Soon and I were presented with a few mushrooms (not the ones Rose had found!) and given instructions about what to do with them: clean well, and fry in butter. I did just that, and they were truly delicious.

Happiness can come in very simple ways. And being in a beautiful place with someone you love; that doesn't do any harm either!

44. ALL SAINTS

I attended at the start of November 2019 two very different cathedral remembrance services, one by accident, the other planned.

The first was in Canterbury Cathedral, where I'd gone expecting the Saturday afternoon Evensong. Instead there was a 'Eucharist of the Commemoration of the Faithful Departed', with the girls' and men's choirs. I glanced down at the programme and was thrilled to see that they would be singing some of Fauré's *Requiem*. It was a dignified and prayerful service, part of which was the naming of the faithful departed, and I thought particularly of my dad and gave thanks for his life. When the girls began to sing the 'Pie Jesu' from the *Requiem* (usually sung by a solo boy chorister!) it was one of those very special 'moments'. There I was still dripping wet in my (almost!) waterproof jacket and trousers after the pouring rain outside, sitting in the choir stalls of Canterbury Cathedral, looking up and around at the beautiful stonework and stained glass windows and in awe, as ever, at the sheer vastness of the building, listening to the voices of angels singing a piece that I've performed myself in that grand venue, thinking about those I've loved that have died; and I said to myself, 'How lucky am I.' Ironically, I'd been thinking about taking Yim Soon to hear a choir in the Cathedral that very evening. In the end we stayed in and watched *Strictly*: I'd had my concert in the Cathedral, and it had been completely free!

The second remembrance service I attended was in St Patrick's Chapel at Westminster Cathedral, an Irish Chaplaincy event to mark the feast of All the Saints of Ireland

126

on November 6th. Bishop Paul McAleenan, who presided, told us that although there are over 300 Irish saints, just four have been officially canonised by the Church. The remainder, including such greats as Patrick and Brigid, were declared saints by the people, in recognition of the lives they lived. Bishop Paul also reminded us that there is no actual word for 'hello' in the Irish language. The usual greeting, rather, is 'God be to you', with the reply being 'God and Mary be to you'. It is a recognition of the sacred in the other person; and it is an attitude, said Bishop Paul, that led to the centrality of hospitality in Irish culture. There was also a nice quote from a W.B. Yeats poem: 'The good will always emerge.'

It was a moving service, attended by a nice cross-section of people; and, very much in keeping with the fine tradition of Irish hospitality, it was followed by tea and cakes, during which many people remarked on what a lovely atmosphere there had been both during the service and subsequently in the café.

The following morning on Radio 4's *Thought for the Day* I was struck by a quote from another poet, the native American Linda Hogan, who speaks of the importance of remembering and honouring our ancestors and writes that, 'You are the result of the love of thousands.'

So for all of those we remember each November, and for countless others un-named; and for all the saints, and for all of those unofficially declared so, I give thanks.

45. LOW LIE THE FIELDS OF ATHENRY

Joy can be found in unexpected places, such as in a prison where hours earlier somebody had taken their own life.

Ellena and I had arrived at HMP Chelmsford for the regular Traveller forum and were informed straight away by the lovely RC chaplains, Merryl and Philomena (affectionately known as Sister P.) about the tragic events of the morning (and suicide is now an all too common occurrence in the prison estate). Philomena was especially shaken, as she had been over to the cell to bless it and to comfort the prison officers who had been on the scene. It was touch and go whether the Traveller forum would go ahead. Any group activity means 'free flow' of prisoners from their cells, and that requires a sufficient number of officers; and some had either gone to the hospital or gone home in distress. In the end it was the only afternoon activity that was allowed to take place in the prison and a large and enthusiastic group of Travellers, some of whom looked *so* young, duly came through the door and greeted us and their mates and took their seats. Merryl and Philomena marked the death of their fellow prisoner with some special prayers and our regular band, McCool Trad, played a mournful ballad before launching, as agreed beforehand, into a couple of lively jigs. It was just what was needed to lift the spirits. The guys began to clap and Philomena got up to dance and she wanted a partner. The young men were all too shy so I seized my chance and took to the floor with a very lively Sr P.

Finn who usually sings with the band hadn't been able to

come so the other members, Nicky, Elaine and Joe had enlisted me to do a few Irish songs and I gladly took the mic. It was an appreciative audience, as it always is in prison, although the men resisted my entreaties to come and sing themselves until one of them got up and took the mic to do a good rendition of a Country and Western number. The warm ambience was further enhanced by the arrival of the food, which, unlike the usual prison fayre, was both plentiful and delicious. It was bacon and cabbage and potatoes, with steamed pudding and custard for dessert. A true feast. There was soda bread too with the meal, and I was touched when one of the guys, having seen that the bread had run out before I'd got there, gave me his slice.

There was time after the food for more music from the wonderful band and there was a request for 'The Fields of Athenry'. I was halfway into the first verse when the Country and Western man strode forward, put his arm around me and sang with me into the mic. And when we got to the chorus the rest of the men were roaring out the words and punching the air. With all that had happened in the prison earlier in the day it was an unforgettable moment of pure joy.

It was time for everyone to be escorted back to their cells. As they left, Ellena handed each person a bag of treats and they all said, as they always do, how grateful they were. And there was one further unexpected gift: Sr P. had for the band members and for Ellena and I a box of chocolates and a card.

I went home that evening feeling completely uplifted.

46. VIVA LA MÚSICA

Music is especially evocative during Advent, although for some people the memories touched can be bittersweet, as I discovered on a prison visit a couple of weeks before Christmas.

We were in Wormwood Scrubs for the regular Irish Chaplaincy Traveller forum and I'd brought my guitar in to play to what turned out to be a *very* lively group! One or two of the younger guys were being a bit overly boisterous but I didn't let it put me off. I just kept singing and I just kept smiling, as I looked around the group making eye contact. It was reassuring to see that a couple of the men were quietly singing along to the Irish songs. I'd planned to lead into a medley of Christmas numbers, both traditional and modern, assuming that everyone would be in the mood for some Christmas music; but was pulled up short when one guy exclaimed, 'We don't want to be reminded of Christmas when we're in here.' 'Can I at least do "Fairytale of New York"?' I pleaded, and happily they relented, and were singing the chorus with gusto. I think I managed to win them over because when it came to the refreshments they were almost fighting each other to make me a cup of tea. I ended up with four! One of which had so much sugar in it, it was almost undrinkable! Not to matter; I was really touched, so too when there was a whip round for mince pies for me, before any leftovers got secreted into jogging trouser pockets to be smuggled back to the cells!

There was a man sitting next to me who had not seemed very happy when I'd been singing and I assumed he just didn't like the songs or didn't like me or whatever! But after the

130

drinks he suddenly said to me, 'You've a queer good voice but this just reminds me of being in the pub.' Another came over to talk to me. He'd been one of those singing along and he was a good bit older than the rest. He explained to me, 'Ah, the young guys get a bit over-excited.' We had a long chat. It was his first time in prison and he said, 'It's like spending twenty-three hours a day in a bathroom.' That was certainly a striking image of the reality of being in prison.

The week before the Scrubs gig I'd been singing in a care home in Kensington for people with dementia, which I always enjoy. I do mainly Irish songs for the benefit of the Irish people there but everyone in what is a very international group of residents appreciates the music. As I was going round greeting people on arrival one of the Irishmen, clearly in a cheeky mood, motioned to the lady next to him and said to me, 'Give her a kiss!'

This group was *very* much up for Christmas songs! People were singing along with the so-familiar melodies; and when it got to 'Jingle Bells' even some of those who are normally quite subdued were joining in and moving their arms, with their faces lighting up in recognition. It was a lovely moment. So too when a Colombian lady (the one I'd been encouraged to kiss at the start) came up to me and said in Spanish, 'The singing was beautiful. May God bless you.'

In the run up to Christmas we did carol singing in two other care homes where we visit Irish people and we would, I'm sure, have been invoking more memories, hopefully positive. Music has such power to both transport us to another time and place, but also to bring together people and cultures.

How blessed I am to have contact with such incredible people in such a rich variety of situations and to have music as one of the means by which we encounter one another and share in our common humanity.

47. IF MUSIC BE THE FOOD OF LOVE

I was struck by two comments about the power of music, one from a ninety-nine-year-old Kerry woman; the other by a young man from Belfast.

One of the carol singing events in care homes mentioned in the last chapter that particularly stood out was at St Teresa's in Wimbledon. Paul, Rory and I were joined by one of our lovely volunteers, Christine, who's originally from Dublin and who had been going faithfully every Friday to chat to the mainly Irish residents (and during the coronavirus pandemic she had continued her contact, with regular phone calls to 'the ladies'). I'd planned a repertoire of Christmas songs, both old and new, but as we were waiting for everyone to arrive, I decided to warm up with some Irish songs. It was immediately clear that this was a group who didn't need any warming up. Everyone was both moved by the music and *moving*. Feet were tapping and arms were waving as people sang along to the familiar tunes. Sheila from Kerry had requested 'The Galway Shawl' in honour of a recently arrived Galwayman and I happily began with that, in honour too of my own dad. And then for Sheila I did a couple of songs from Kerry: 'The Black Velvet Band' and 'Golden Jubilee'. For the Dubliners present we sang 'Molly Malone'; and for the several people from Cork there was 'Whiskey in the Jar' (not literally, I'm afraid!). The house was absolutely ROCKING; and anyway, who needs whiskey to have a good time! I slowed it down with 'Sweet Sixteen', before launching into the Christmas set. It was quite simply the most joyful and uplifting experience imaginable.

One of the Cork ladies confided to me later that she was

normally quite shy but had so much enjoyed the singing and dancing. And as for Sheila, she said (and I remembered it word for word, it was so heart-warming):

'We were expecting carol singers and then you fellas turned up! The singing was heavenly. You had us lifted out of our chairs and flying through the air like angels. You've made our Christmas perfect.'

Straight after the excitement of Christmas, we were working hard on our second St Brigid's concert, at St James's Church Piccadilly at the end of January 2020, which would have a host of talented performers, ranging in age from the young people of the London Celtic Youth Orchestra to the more mature members of the Irish Elders' Choir. I received a message from one of those on the bill, Belfast-born actor Anton Thompson-McCormick, who I had bumped into 'by chance' a few months earlier in a back-street bar in Lewes:

'January 31st will be a delight, people coming together and celebrating the good things - how else to start the decade?'

I also at that time was sent the copy of a letter addressed to me that had been sent to the ICPO (Irish Council for Prisoners Overseas) office in Maynooth from a man in a prison in the North of England. He wrote:

'After reading your article in the ICPO Christmas newsletter 2019 I was impressed that the guitar you had used for the last twenty-four years had been put to more good use by taking it into Wormwood Scrubs,' and he went on to ask if I could come and perform to him and the other twenty-five Irish prisoners there, explaining that 'My friends and I are very keen on the idea and it would give us a more positive vibe to take forward.' He ended with the words, 'Thank you for sharing your story and in fact your guitar.' I was incredibly touched by that and it shows again that we just never know the impact we might have on somebody's life.

I resolved at that start of another new year that if music was indeed the food of love then we were to PLAY ON!

48. A NICE CUP OF TEA

When I arrived at the train station one Monday morning in January I was greeted by volunteers from the Samaritans handing out tea bags to commuters. I still had in a cupboard the one I'd been given the year before!

It was the day of the year on which people are said to be most likely to be depressed. It's the third full week back at work after Christmas, it's still dark in the morning, and credit card bills are coming through (and, yes, the flip side of getting paid earlier in December is that the money runs out sooner in January!). I was actually feeling pretty up-beat that day. I was relishing the cold, frosty snap we were having; and was glad to be back into the routine of work following my usual start of the year inertia. The previous Monday had been my personal low-point, and as I'd sat on the train that dark, grey, gloomy morning asking myself what the point of it all was, I'd assumed that must be the 'most depressed' day and wondered why the Samaritans hadn't given us a tea bag this year! I'm fortunate that I've never experienced deep depression but each year the beginning of January is a bit of a struggle. I cling on to the knowledge that I've been there before and somehow I made it through in one piece.

The point of the tea bag, according to the Samaritans, is that it's good to talk to someone. But let's face it, for some people that's easier said than done. For myself, I realise that following the excesses of the Christmas period I crave time on my own to just be still and to rest and to hibernate. I was lucky to be able to leave the office on a couple of occasions and go off to cafés in Camden where I got on quietly with my work on my laptop, whilst having a very nice cup of tea.

When in Dublin I sometimes enjoy the warm hospitality of the Mercy sisters in Baggot Street in the house where Catherine McAuley founded the order in the nineteenth century, and one of the members of which is our lovely Sr Moira. I'm always struck by Catherine's last words to her sisters as she lay dying: 'Be sure you have a comfortable cup of tea for them when I am gone.' Ever since, the comfortable cup of tea has been a symbol of the welcome and the caring relationships at the heart of Catherine McAuley's Mercy vision.

Whenever we have a visitor at the Irish Chaplaincy the first question they are usually asked is, 'Would you like a cup of tea?' There is barely an hour goes by at the Chaplaincy without someone putting the kettle on: not to mention Gerry appearing at the door with his offer of chunky chocolate cookies, and Liz and Breda their pastries, and Fiona her mini muffins, and Pat her leftover cakes, and Paul his Friday bars of chocolate. It wasn't a huge hardship to work in that office, and how we missed the Friday chocolate during lockdown!

Another of the perks of my job, apart from unlimited tea and sweet things, is getting invited to special events at the Irish Embassy. I'd been there twice in the previous week, the second time for the celebration of twenty-five years of Treskellion Theatre, founded by another Irish Chaplaincy volunteer, Gerry Molumby. I was excited to see in the reception area Eilish and eleven of her talented young musicians from the London Celtic Youth Orchestra. I got chatting to a couple of London Irish ladies, one of whom commented, 'They make a great noise, don't they.' I handed them a flyer for our St Brigid's concert and said, 'Just wait till you hear forty-three of them next week, and with their four harps and their dancers!' And talking of Irish dancing, we had the incredible pleasure later on of seeing world title-winning Joe McGowan in action; his shoes making a wonderful noise on the bare wooden floor of the Embassy ballroom.

LOOKING AHEAD WITH HOPE

A couple of weeks before, I was invited to speak at a couple of Masses at a church in London. I'd been asked to share about the experience of going on retreat, and I also planned to talk about the work of the Chaplaincy. I encouraged people to find places of stillness in their daily and weekly lives, whether it be going into the local park for ten minutes to look at the trees and listen to the birds, or getting up half an hour earlier in the morning to sit quietly in a favourite armchair with a cup of tea. I realised that I needed to follow my own advice and so got into just such a routine each day, sitting in the early morning darkness in a comfy chair with a nice cup of tea.

When spending a year in Seoul with my family from 1999-2000 my regular retreat day was a monthly twenty-four hours spent with the Columbans, a highly entertaining bunch of Irish missionary priests. And, fittingly, those nine priests who had founded the Irish Chaplaincy back in 1957 happened to be Columbans. The Columban house in downtown Seoul was a bit of an oasis for me. There were back issues of the *Irish Times* in the garden room, and there was REAL tea! I would arrive there fairly exhausted from the demands of three young children, teaching English six days a week and generally being in an unfamiliar place (rich as that experience is) and one of the guys Pat Muldoon, who was especially good to me, said on every visit, 'Be nice to yourself'.

I think that's ultimately the message of the Samaritans when giving out their tea bags on the third Monday back at work after Christmas; or our fantastic people at the Irish Chaplaincy, whether out on their pastoral visits or when putting on the kettle and dishing out little treats: let's be kind to one another.

49. ONCE IN A VERY BLUE MOON

Music has a particular power to transport us to another time and place, and one of the songs performed at our St Brigid's concert had me back in the cosy living-room of a house in a village in East Kent in 1992.

For the second year running the Irish Chaplaincy was hosting a 'Celebration of Irish music, poetry and dancing' at St James's church, Piccadilly and we had assembled an impressive and varied line-up. First on stage were forty-three members of the London Celtic youth Orchestra, directed by the amazing Eilish Byrne-Whelehan and they had the audience of several hundred clapping and tapping their feet. They were followed by a host of talented solo singers, dancers and poets; as well as an ensemble, the Luckpenny Ceílí band. There were many special moments, although the highlight for me was the tribute to Mary Black by Lucy Winkett who is Rector of St James's.

As explained earlier, Lucy and I first met when she came to spend six months at L'Arche Kent, prior to going to theological college. She was an assistant in Cana, the L'Arche house in the village of Eythorne, between Canterbury and Dover, where I was House Leader for three years before I got married at the end of 1992 (and Lucy says she still thinks of me as her boss!). There we were, sharing life together as part of a group of a dozen or so people with and without learning disabilities and it was a delight to have Lucy with us. There was a particular routine in those days. We'd all eat together in the evening around a large wooden table, then go into the living-room for a simple but very intimate time of prayer, during which I'd normally lead a couple of songs that people could join in with easily. Then one time after the prayer Lucy produced her own guitar and sang a song she'd just learnt. I thought, 'Oh my God, she sings as well!' It was one of the songs that she'd been listening to on a Mary Black album; and she subsequently learnt all the songs on that LP. The song she sang that night was 'Once in a very blue moon'. And it blew me away.

I'd had a similar experience four years earlier when coming for my first visit to L'Arche Kent. I'd arrived at Little Ewell, the big old house in the village of Barfreston, near Eythorne: the first house of L'Arche in the U.K. when it opened in 1974. I showed up just in time for the evening meal, and I still remember what we ate. Food, like music, can invoke strong memories. It was home-made tuna pizza, enjoyed with a group of about twenty people around a huge oval-shaped wooden table, with great banter to go with the delicious food. I was thinking, '*What* an interesting bunch of people.' And following the meal we processed into the large living-room with its richly polished wooden floor for a simple but incredibly moving time of prayer, after which a guy called Gerry O'Riordan picked up a guitar and sang some James Taylor songs. I knew it was the place for me.

Fast forward to 2020 in St James's Church in the heart of London. Lucy comes on in the second half of the concert, and she's sitting at the grand piano (a last-minute decision to use that rather than guitar). And she sings the song she sang in the Cana living-room in 1992. And it is so beautiful. I'd shed a few tears already when I'd heard her practise it earlier in the day. She'd asked my advice about what to do as a second number. I'd said, 'Do whatever you like, as long as you do "Once in a very blue moon"!' My eyes were dry for the 'actual' performance but it's such a privilege to be surrounded by such goodness. And it's a privilege as well to finish the concert with a couple of my own songs. I wrote 'Twenty Years Ago' for my wonderful wife Yim Soon for our twentieth wedding anniversary; with Lucy having sung at our wedding. 'Fare ye Well', the final song of the concert, was written for a special L'Arche event in 2012: a 'Thank you' celebration after I'd finished as Community Leader of L'Arche Kent and was preparing to go away for a six-month sabbatical. One of the verses is based on an old Irish blessing:

Fare ye well my dear friends
May our paths be straight, our footsteps firm
May the wind be always on our back, and the sun upon
     our face
May the road rise up to meet us and until we meet again
May God hold each one gently in the palm of His hand
Fare ye well my dear friends, fare ye well.

I hope we'll be back at St James's, post-coronavirus, for another St Brigid's concert. And I hope that Lucy will sing that song again.

50. LIVING WITH DEMENTIA

Our society has a tendency to view old age as a problem and the elderly as a burden on the state; and dementia tends to be seen in an especially negative light. We hear, for example, that somebody 'suffers' from dementia, we use words like 'decline', and there is often a perception that the person is somehow no longer there, or that they are almost an empty shell.

I was in a care home and was chatting to an Irish lady who lived there alongside her husband, who appeared, on the surface at least, to be rather unresponsive. I was impressed by the level of care and attention he was receiving from his wife of many years as she held up a beaker of water to his lips and helped him to chew on a biscuit. 'He used to have a great brain,' she confided to me, 'now it's all in pieces.'

It's all a bit more real for me these days as my dear, wonderful mum is living with dementia. Her short-term memory has got a lot worse and yet her lovely nature continues to shine through; in the way, for example, she speaks to the staff: 'Thanks ever so much love,' and, 'God love you.' She still takes a keen interest in what's going on around her, and about which she still makes pertinent and humorous little comments. And we still have a good laugh together, even if things get increasingly a bit mixed up in her brain. Sometimes she seems to be back in her native Newry, and occasionally when I phone she seems to think that I might be one of her brothers. And when I saw her just after Christmas 2019 she appeared to remember the name of only the eldest of her five grandchildren, the others being variously referred to as 'the other fella' or 'the wee fella'. Although, if truth be told, when it comes to remembering names, which of us is not on that slippery slope! I arrived on the last day of that post-Christmas visit to find a sizeable group of the women in the dining-room in rapt attention: it was the bingo. I asked mum if she wanted to go to her room for a quiet chat. 'Ah, after the bingo,' she said. She was 100 per cent focussed and there was nothing at all mixed up in her brain as she went on to win the next full house!

I came across an interesting book by John Swinton, professor of practical theology and pastoral care at the University of Aberdeen: *Dementia: Living in the Memories of God*. In the Introduction, entitled 'Being Loved for who I Am', Swinton recalls how he was asked once on a TV programme: 'If you ended up having dementia, how would you like to be treated?' His answer was, 'I hope I will be loved and cared for just for who I am, even if who I am is difficult for me and for others.' He goes on to raise the interesting point that the question of who I am is not necessarily straightforward when our brains are functioning 'normally', let alone when I may have forgotten who I thought I was.

In a later chapter, 'Becoming friends of time', he speaks of the simple act of being present to another person. He tells a story, entitled 'The sacrament of the present moment', in which John Goldingay, a seminary professor of Old Testament in California, invited his students to come and have pancakes with him and his beloved wife Ann who was in an advanced stage of dementia. He encouraged them to speak to Ann even if she might appear unresponsive and he said, 'She probably won't remember you afterwards, but in that moment she will appreciate you.' That story reminded me of a visit I made to a lovely Galway woman who lives in a care home and who I'd seen a few times before. As I entered her room she said to me, 'I don't know who you are but it's very nice to see you!'

Goldingay describes his journey with Ann in his book *Walk On* and writes, 'It can seem now as if Ann is almost gone ... there is so little of her here now.' Yet, he is challenged by a care giver who sees Ann in a different way. This person enjoyed simply sitting with Ann over the course of a year and remarked, 'Ann's spirit ministers to my spirit.'

There's a story in John Swinton's book about another man caring for a wife with Alzheimer's. This person had been a successful, and very busy, businessman, but now he devoted himself entirely to the care of his wife: feeding her, bathing her. One night she woke him and, as if emerging from a fog for a moment, said, 'Darling, I just want to say thank you for all you're doing for me,' and then she fell back into the fog.

Dementia raises interesting questions about who we are at our core, about what it means to be human, and about what makes for a 'valued' and 'worthwhile' life. It's interesting as well to examine our assumptions that a person living with dementia is somehow in decline and suffering and going 'downhill'. If I ask myself that question that John Swinton was asked in the TV interview, 'How would I like to be treated if I had dementia', my answer might be: with love, and with dignity and respect. But then again, it might not be too far from Swinton's response, 'Loved and cared for just for who I am'. I hope as well that there will be people who will simply sit with me and be fully present in that moment, even if I may not remember them with my conscious mind the moment they've walked out the door.

51. SPRINGTIME

There was an exciting milestone a few days into March: I was able to sit out in the garden with a cup of tea for the first time.

I'd got back from my Saturday morning club cycle ride. It was the first one I'd done for ages, what with a different, benignly-named storm every weekend; and, as it turned out, it was one of the last, due to the pandemic that was about to change our lives. I was enjoying my post-exercise brew on the bench at the bottom of the garden. It's in a nicely secluded spot, hidden from view of the house by some strategically placed shrubs, and as I sat there I was overwhelmed and overjoyed by the gentle beauty of the birdsong and the sense of the earth coming back to life after its winter slumber. We're blessed in our garden with masses of daffodils, the fruits of many years' worth of autumnal bulb-planting, and they are joined in their magnificent yellowness by the forsythia, another faithful harbinger of Spring. The snowdrops, which I've concentrated around a gnarled old apple tree, and the crocuses had been and gone, but the small anemones were out, their purple (along with that of the heather) contrasting nicely with the yellow of the daffodils. The grape hyacinths were almost there, the tulips were on their way, and the clematis montana, draped along a fence, that looked so barren and lifeless just a fortnight before, was poised to burst into a sea of pink.

A garden is a place of pleasure and respite at any time of year and I've designed ours so that there is interest, and even colour, in virtually each of the twelve months, but Spring is perhaps a particular occasion to marvel at the miracle of creation and to behold the endless cycle of death and new life. It always seems to me a little incongruous that the Church chooses this time of the year to mark Lent, a period traditionally associated with fasting and other self-denial. I've never been very good at fasting: not from food, at any rate, although there *are* other forms of fasting. In the dark days of January, and following the excesses of Christmas, a period of abstinence is rather welcome. But with new life literally springing up all around, I want to be outside and to rejoice and celebrate this annual miracle. And I'm struck that the origin of the word Lent is in the Old English 'lencten' which simply means 'springtime', and the West Germanic 'langitinaz', meaning 'lengthening of the day'.

I enjoy reading each year the daily Lenten reflections of Brian Draper, and he encourages us, amongst other things, to take deep breaths and to notice: both what's going on around us and what might be going on within. So I try during Lent to notice a bit more, as well as to regain that sense of wonder that young children seem to have so naturally. Such noticing might be the song of a bird, or the trees coming back into bud, or the person who might be in need. I attempt to practise a little bit of self-denial. I might not do that very successfully; but I try not to beat myself up over it! I'm also inspired by the words of the prophet Isaiah who suggests (and I paraphrase from Chapter 58) that God does not desire us to be miserable while we fast; rather that the kind of fasting which is pleasing to God is sharing our bread with the hungry, welcoming the stranger, and freeing those who are oppressed. And, interestingly, Isaiah goes on to say that having done the above, 'You shall be like a watered garden.'

Some years ago, in the Springtime, I was getting ready to walk with my friend James on the Camino, the ancient pilgrimage route across the North of Spain. He was carrying in his (very large) rucksack a stove and a billy can so that we could make tea along the way. James is Australian and they do that kind of thing in the outback! We gained something of

144

a reputation on the Camino, amongst other things, for being the two guys who would stop at random places en route to make a cup of tea. One day, early in the morning, we were sitting on a bench outside the municipal hostel in Nájera, where we'd 'slept' with 120 other people in one single room of bunk beds. The water was boiling on the stove, the sun was just beginning to rise over the trees, the birds were singing, and there was the most delightful sound of water from the fast-flowing river nearby. We were sitting in reverent silence, and then James said, 'Another day in paradise.'

When I returned from the Camino I tried each day when I got up in the morning and opened the curtains to say to myself, 'Another day in paradise', and I managed it for a few weeks. Those words also inspired a song, 'El Camino'.

Our world is filled with pain and fear and uncertainty, especially so at the time of the coronavirus. Our world is also filled with beauty, especially in the Springtime, if only we have 'Ears to hear, and eyes to see'. I will continue to enjoy those cups of tea in the garden. And I will try afresh to see each day as another one in paradise.

52. A VERY DIFFERENT KIND OF ST PATRICK'S DAY

On 17 March 2020, our daughter Miran was due to fly to Seoul, and then spend five months travelling in Asia. She was to return to Korea in May to meet up with Yim Soon, who was going out to her homeland for a few weeks as part of her 60th birthday celebrations. The 60th birthday is a big event in Korea: historically, people were lucky if they made it that far. Yim Soon's actual birthday in 2020, the date varying each year according to the lunar calendar, happened to be on 17 March. There was a big party due to take place in the evening at Faith House, the L'Arche house in Canterbury where we'd first met thirty-one years before. She had requested Irish music, and John-Paul and I were going to revive our old fiddle and guitar combination.

Miran didn't go to Seoul that day; I didn't catch the train to London; and Yim Soon was spending her birthday in quarantine, coughing a bit and having a temperature. At least she thought so: she wasn't able to check it, since everywhere was, like with pasta and toilet roll, sold out of thermometers! She was sending me her food and drink orders via Facebook Messenger, and I was delivering to the door! Miran and I, meanwhile, were in self-isolation for two weeks. She was bitterly disappointed that she wasn't on her way to an exotic beach somewhere, and had already announced that self-isolation was 'SO BORING', although for me it was a gift to have her at home at that time.

LOOKING AHEAD WITH HOPE

And it was St Patrick's Day. But the parades and events in London and elsewhere had been cancelled due to the rapidly spreading coronavirus. The night before, there was to have been the reception at the Irish Embassy which is always a lively do. A couple of years before, they gave out little sprigs of shamrock for us to pin on. It brought me back to my childhood, when, on St Patrick's Day, my sister and I would have various green, white and gold badges and floppy bits of shamrock pinned to us by our mum and sent off to school. It was always so floppy: it never really survived the journey from Ireland in an envelope! It was pretty embarrassing turning up to school each year on 17 March sporting a floppy bit of shamrock, even though, with it being a Catholic school in Coventry, lots of other children were similarly adorned. There's always so much that can embarrass a child: you don't need your mum doing additional weird stuff to you! Well, two years before at the Embassy I'd worn my floppy shamrock with pride, and it even got me into a conversation with a Cork man on the train home from London. It turned out that his wife's best friend from childhood was someone I knew.

Sadly, our conversations with random strangers, or even with friends and family, were now going to be largely restricted to 'virtual' ones. But human beings would adapt: they always have done. And the human spirit is strong. Yes, some people bought more than they needed in the supermarkets, driven perhaps by the very real anxiety brought about by an unknown threat. But there would also be many unseen acts of kindness. I was touched by pictures of people in Italy, confined to their flats, standing on the balcony and singing the same song as the others in their block. And I came across a lovely video on Facebook, entitled 'Quarantine creativity', of three Georgian students trapped in their Italian apartment and singing traditional folk songs from their country with the words changed to things like: 'We wash our hands, we wash our face, we wear face masks, and sometimes we swig spirits to scare corona … with god's grace we will survive this rotten corona!'

Covid-19 unleashed a wave of creativity; and YouTube was to be filled with 'coronavirus' songs. One of them was my own, 'Corona blues', complete with video. This was partly inspired by the images of Italians on their balconies during isolation holding up banners proclaiming 'Andrà tutto bene', all shall be well

We were in new territory as nations and as a human race, and during those first rather unsettling days of lockdown, there was no telling when it would all end. But end it would, and I was curious to see what we would have learnt as individuals and as a society and which of those forced changes in lifestyle we might wish to continue with post-virus. We had found out surprisingly quickly that we don't necessarily have to pack ourselves onto a train in the morning to go to work, and that we can cut down on air travel quite easily if we really want to. We discovered more and more ways to be connected virtually. But there's no perfect substitute for face-to-face encounter: to be with another person in the flesh, to laugh together, to cry together, to sing together, or just to be silent together. Many isolated people became even more isolated in the lockdown, and it wasn't just the elderly. I hope we came to see afresh how we need to come together as groups, whether that's singing in a choir, or cycling with a club, or attending a religious service or a lunch club, or going to a concert or a sporting event; or taking part in a parade whilst wearing, with great pride, a floppy bit of shamrock.

53. SAVED BY THE CHOCOLATE CAFÉ

There was just one café left in Canterbury where you could sit down inside and drink your tea, and it saved me in more ways than one.

I'd begun Day Three of enforced home-working determined to stay positive, even if I was anxious about my beloved wife Yim Soon, who still had some COVID-19 symptoms, and pleading with God to keep her safe. It was a blessing that I had plenty of work to get stuck into, although I was increasingly impeded by not being able to get remote access to my office files. I needed Dan! Dan is our IT guy at the Irish Chaplaincy and I'd always assumed that he lived in London but when about a year went by after me starting at the Chaplaincy and I still hadn't met him I was wondering if he really existed, or whether he might in fact be a virtual Dan! Well, he is very much a real person, and he lives in Budapest. And if I have issues with my laptop he can sort them out via 'TeamViewer', which allows for remote access. It's an amazing business. I send him a password and then sit back and watch as the cursor runs back and forth on my computer screen and various weird and wonderful pages are opened and closed and things get clicked or unclicked, and the problem gets solved.

The trouble was, my home internet wasn't allowing me to access TeamViewer, so I would have to get online somewhere else (and I was supposed to be in self-isolation!). I cycled down to the library and found a place to sit that was the requisite number of metres from any fellow human being and

149

spent a pleasant few hours working whilst waiting for Dan to do his magic tricks. I got a message from him eventually to say that he'd been really busy and could we do it at 6 p.m. The library would be closing then, and there was a rather ominous announcement that it would remain shut until further notice. I really *was* going to be stuck at home in the weeks ahead. But surely a café would still be open. I cycled back into the centre of Canterbury in time for 6 o'clock and found, to my dismay, that one after another café was only doing takeaway drinks. But lo and behold there was one place still standing. Eleto Chocolate Café is a slightly quirky little place not far from the Cathedral with nice views of the spires rising over the rooftops of the (now closed) cafés opposite. I used to go there sometimes for 1 to 1 meetings when I was at L'Arche. The young man behind the counter confirmed that yes, they were still open (till 9 p.m.), and yes, I could sit inside, and yes, there was Wi-Fi.

I found a table all to myself, which wasn't difficult as the place was almost deserted. I connected to the Wi-Fi and sent Dan the TeamViewer password and he got to work. And I sat back, with my view of the beautiful, illuminated spires of the Cathedral, and drank my tea, and began to write a letter to my friend Mike in Rome. And I noticed the music that was playing: 'Blue Monday' by New Order, one of the songs I used to dance to as a just-left-home eighteen-year-old. Wow! And it was followed by other early 80s hits by The Police, The Human League, Tears for Fears (it's a 'Mad World' indeed!), David Bowie. I looked at the three people behind the counter, all of them in their 20s. What was going on? Was this just for me, to lift my spirits at this anxious time? Well, lift my sprits it most certainly did. I was giving Mike, who's a similar age to me, a running commentary of the playlist as I scribbled. And then I saw on the laptop that Dan had produced his final flourish and I was once again able to access my office files: pretty crucial with the prospect of months of home-working ahead. And just at that moment there began the dramatic cello intro. to ELO's 'Mr Blue Sky', which will always bring a tingle to my spine: 'Sun is shining in the sky, there ain't a cloud in sight; it's stopped raining, everybody's in the play, and don't you know, it's a beautiful new day; hey, hey, hey.'

I declared to Mike the words that had been commonly seen on sheets draped from apartments in Italy, and which I was to use, in various languages, in the video for my song 'Corona Blues':

Andrà tutto bene ... All shall be well.

I rose rather reluctantly to go back out into the cold and dark and largely empty streets and to uncertain times ahead. And as I made my leave of Eleto Chocolate Café I said to the three lovely young people there: 'Great music, and you've saved me.'

54. ETERNAL CHRISTMAS?

Everything was different during the lockdown, and it was a very different kind of Sunday. I would usually get up a bit later when it got to Sunday morning so as to fully recover from the busy week in London just passed and to rest in preparation for the busy week to come, but as the lyrics of ELO's 'Mr Blue Sky' go, 'It's a beautiful new day, hey, hey, hey', and following what seemed like months of rain the sky really had been so blue in the past days, so I rose early and went for a first (socially-distanced) walk of the day. There was now lots of time for walking!

I used to go the gym on Sunday afternoon, and later to church, but both of those were now out, together with other activities that had been fixed points in my week, like choir on a Tuesday evening and my cycling club on a Saturday morning. I headed up instead to the attractive campus of Kent University, perched on a hill overlooking the city and with wonderful views of the Cathedral, and I kept seeing people I knew. Sammy from the cycling club drove past and gave me a big wave. Gosia from L'Arche was out for a walk with her two school-age children and we had a little chat (several yards apart). She said, 'We're going to learn new skills in this time.' 'Like what?' I enquired. 'Well,' she said with a smile, 'how to be with people twenty-four hours a day!'

Yes, how to be with people round the clock, I reflected, with the amount of people in my house having gone suddenly from two to four: our daughter Miran not travelling in Asia, and our youngest son Sean sent home from uni to revise for exams which would be on-line. I carried on up the hill and reached a campus which was now largely free of students but with plenty of locals … walking! I was delighted to see the Alexopoulos family who we've known for years, having similar aged children, and whose Big Greek Christmas party is always one of the hottest tickets in Canterbury during the festive season. They were there for a Mother's Day trip out and were drinking takeaway coffee on a picnic bench. We had a long conversation and Eleftheria voiced something that I'd been thinking myself earlier in the day: 'It's like Christmas: all the family are home, and everywhere is closed!' 'Exactly,' I said, 'it's Christmas every day now, without the presents!'

And yet, I got to thinking, what *were* the gifts that we might receive at such an unusual time? Could it be that one of the things we fear most, and try our utmost to 'fill', could be one of the greatest gifts, i.e. time itself. There had been a 'Thought for the Day' at the start of the week from one of my favourite speakers, John Bell of the Iona community, and this is precisely what he seemed to be saying and he finished by wondering whether the period of lockdown could be an opportunity to 'love into life' some of the neglected aspects within ourselves.

I was still unsure how I would make the best use of the weeks or months ahead. Up until that point I had enjoyed having a bit more time to write, and was heartened by the encouraging comments I was receiving from people in response to what I was writing, not to mention the sense of connection. I'd also written a letter to somebody that I'd been meaning to write to for about two years! And I had just discovered a live stream of Evening Prayer of the Taizé community in the South of France, one of my favourite places in the world. Mid-way through the Taizé prayer that day there was a group chat call from our eldest son Kieran to wish Yim Soon 'Happy Mother's Day'. There we were on the screen, the five of us, and I still had on my laptop the white-robed figures of the Taizé brothers at prayer and could hear their singing. And I was together with nearly 4,000 others from around the world who were also listening in, and sending messages of hope. It was a special moment of communion and connection. Whether it be Christmas or any other time, what more precious gift is there.

55. THE WORLD IS STILL A HANDKERCHIEF

The seafront at Herne Bay was eerily quiet. I was on the second day of a newly established rhythm, which included starting work early in the morning and finishing mid-afternoon to go for a long bike ride. The day before, I'd taken the direct route to the sea: through Clowes Wood to a deserted Whitstable. This time I would follow a familiar loop through Thorndon Woods to Herne Bay, then along the coast and back from Whitstable to Canterbury via the Crab & Winkle Line. When I reached Herne Bay I had a sudden urge to drink a latte by the beach. I just needed to do something kind of 'normal'. I was delighted to find a petrol station open on the otherwise closed up High Street and there was a Costa coffee machine inside, so I happily prepared my latte and also bought a chocolate flapjack (I thought, 'Let's go mad!'). This was to become a familiar ritual in the weeks ahead.

I wandered down towards the beach and found an empty bench, which wasn't difficult as there was barely a soul on what is usually a bustling stretch of promenade by the pier. I sat and sipped my latte in the gorgeous sunshine and I looked out at the calm, blue sea. And then two young guys in shorts and T-shirts appeared nearby and began filming themselves doing some dance moves in unison which culminated in one of them doing a back flip onto the beach! They were laughing and enjoying themselves so much as they went through various takes, and it was lovely to watch. As I made to cycle off, I said to them, 'Thanks for that.' And then I noticed the emblem on the T-shirt of Mr Back Somersault: Coventry City F.C. 'Are you a Coventry fan?' I asked. You don't see many of those down in East Kent; and I can't say I'm really one myself but it's a sort of link with the hometown, and I knew they were having a great season, on course for a second promotion in three years, sitting on top of League 1 at the point where the leagues got frozen.

In answer to my question he said, 'No, I play for Coventry.' And then it clicked: 'Oh, are you the guy who went to Simon Langton?' (the school in Canterbury that my children went to). He confirmed that he was. 'Do you know Kieran and Sean Gilmore?' 'Yeah, I know Sean,' he said. We had a really nice exchange, and I remarked to him with a smile, 'So this is how you're keeping in shape!' He must have been practising for his next goal celebration!

I told the story excitedly to Sean and Miran when I got home. Sean had played in the school team with Sam McCallum, who went on to become left-back for Coventry City, and told me how he 'always hit the ball so cleanly'. And Miran said, 'Oh, they were doing a TikTok dance.' It's a thing, apparently. A group of people do some dance moves in unison and post it on a TikTok site.

I was reminded yet again of that Spanish expression I'd learnt when walking on the Camino: 'El mundo es un pañuelo', the world is a handkerchief. I was happy to see that, even in the strange and isolating period of lockdown, it still was.

56. FAMINE OR FEAST

I never thought I'd live to see empty supermarket shelves in the UK; or having to queue up to even enter the store.

When the coronavirus was prompting the first wave of panic-buying I went to my big Sainsburys in the evening to get a few things and was shocked by what I found. As I walked rather forlornly up and down aisle after aisle of bare shelves, I said with a smile to a man who was coming up the other way and carrying a similarly empty basket, 'I think we left it too late!' He smiled back as he replied, 'But we're not going to starve, are we!'. I managed to find a few things. They weren't really the items I was looking for, but it was enough: it was more than enough.

I was reminded of a trip I made to a communist-era Prague in the 80s. I went into a shop to buy some food and they had one kind of bread and one kind of cheese and also some tomatoes. I sat outside on a bench, thrilled to find myself on the other side of the infamous 'Iron Curtain', and struck by seeing that people there were just people, like anywhere; and I tucked into one of the most delicious loaves of bread I'd ever tasted (rye flour, with caraway seeds), and the cheese was lovely and the tomatoes were big and juicy. It was a true feast. Years later, I told that story to a Polish friend who remarked, 'You were lucky to get cheese and tomatoes!' In her childhood, forming queues to get into shops that might be largely empty was completely normal.

I'd left home early one morning to buy bread (I'd learnt my lesson!). On the way down to our Sainsburys Local I saw that the door of the Cornish Pasty shop was open with a sign proclaiming 'Free'. The owner had put up a little table with loaves of bread that had reached their sell-by date and I've never been so happy to be given something for free. On closer examination I saw that it was Eastern European rye bread, and I had just on the way there been thinking of that time in Prague: a true moment of serendipity, or call it what you will. I ate it that evening with cheese, and it made a great meal.

It seemed somehow apt that the pandemic should have coincided with the season of Lent, a time associated with fasting. Although I'm not very good at fasting, I like the concept of the famine before the feast which is still taken especially seriously in the Eastern Church, and during Advent as well as Lent. At both periods I always try to abstain from alcohol but never wholly successfully! This time around, we were just a few days into Lent when our youngest son had a sporting success: when spectator sport, and indeed sport itself, was another of those things we just took for granted. Yim Soon and I had a glass of wine to celebrate; it just seemed the right thing to do. But the following weekend we decided to open another bottle, partly as we had quite a few in stock. And now it's confession time. Yim Soon, having followed closely the early coronavirus developments in her native Korea, was way ahead of the game when it came to stockpiling. Back in February she had raided our local Aldi for toilet paper, pasta, a wide selection of hand wash and sanitiser products, and...red wine! ('Darling, don't you think you're over-reacting a bit!'). If anyone complained to me that they couldn't find hand-wash in the shops I'd say, 'Sorry, it's all under a bed in our house!' But with Yim Soon getting ill, the remainder of the emergency wine supply went untouched and we managed to make it to the end of Lent in a state of imposed fasting.

We opened a bottle when we got to Easter, although it was a somewhat subdued affair, in part due to all the churches, or at least the church buildings, being closed. Yet, in the midst of those anxious and extraordinary times, just to be able to look out at the Spring colours in the garden and to see the trees coming into bud again, to be given a loaf of bread by a stranger, to simply be alive: those were things worthy of a feast.

57. PAM DODDS RIP

Zoom calls quickly become a part of the 'new normal', and I even participated in my first Zoom remembrance service.

Pam Dodds was born in Canterbury in 1958 and she came in 1981 to live at Faith House, the newly-opened L'Arche house in Canterbury. I moved into Faith House at the start of 1989 and in May of that year there came L'Arche UK's first ever Korean assistant and the woman who was to become my wife, Yim Soon.

Pam had died alone in her flat, and there were thirty-seven of her friends gathered for the service, some from L'Arche and some from St Thomas', the Catholic church in Canterbury where Pam was a well-known and well-loved member of the parish. Indeed there must have been about forty people present as some of the Zoom windows had two people in them. It seems that twenty-five is the limit for one Zoom screen so that there was an over-spill onto a second screen. And how Pam would have been touched by so many people coming together to sing, to pray and to share memories of her. It was lovely to see old faces, all of us brought together by Pam.

When it got to my turn I explained how my bedroom at Faith House had been directly underneath Pam's and mentioned, rather diplomatically, that I knew well what Pam's favourite records were. The reality was that Pam would play the same three records *very* loudly: and not just the same three records but the same bits of the same three records: *very* loudly! I liked Pam, and I wasn't really bothered by her 'feistiness', and I suppose I must have found a way to cope with the noise coming from above. Human beings are very adaptable, which we were to find at the time of the coronavirus.

Pam didn't find it easy to live with others and in the early 90s she announced that she wanted to leave L'Arche and was supported to move into her own flat. She retreated somewhat into her own, rather troubled, world in the ensuing years and I was delighted when, much later, L'Arche was approached by social services to see if Pam could be given a bit of support again. It was decided that Pam would spend a couple of hours each week with Yim Soon, so Pam came to our house on Tuesday afternoons and she and Yim Soon would drink tea and eat cake and chat and watch a few episodes of *Last of the Summer Wine*. And Ian, one of those at the service, told of how excited Pam was when she visited him in Yorkshire and he took her to Holmfirth where the show was filmed and how they had tea in 'Sid's café'.

Occasionally I would be working from home on a Tuesday and it was special to connect again with Pam and she always asked how my mum was and she always gave me the latest news from her dear friends Janet and Maurice. And I would enjoy hearing the raucous chuckles coming from the living-room as Pam watched her favourite sit-com.

Pam counted many Catholic priests amongst her circle of acquaintances, and was in regular correspondence with several bishops. I was once chatting with her outside Canterbury Cathedral following a big ecumenical service and she spotted Derek Warlock, then Catholic Archbishop of Liverpool. Pam grabbed me and pulled me over to introduce me to her old friend Derek! And she was so happy when another old friend Nick Hudson, who had been an assistant priest in Canterbury in the late 1980s, was made a bishop.

I ended my sharing about Pam with a favourite memory, also on a clerical theme. My friend Richard arrived at L'Arche as an eighteen-year-old in April 1989 and was living at Little Ewell, another of the houses of L'Arche Kent. His House

Leader Maria sent him over to Faith House one day for a visit. Richard was in his Goth phase and so this tall young guy turned up wearing black jeans, a black shirt, large black winkle-picker boots, hair standing up, and around his neck a huge cross. Pam didn't always take kindly to new people but she was all over Richard: the reason, it turned out later; she thought he was a priest!

Thank you Pam. Your life was a gift. May God bless you.

58. SACRED SPACES

A picture posted on Facebook by an old friend from L'Arche reminded me of the importance of special places that we can return to, whether physically, virtually or in the imagination.

It was the Zen garden at Orval, a Trappist monastery in Belgium where many L'Arche retreats took place. We were there a few times with our children when they were young and I have a particular memory of them in that garden. Together with the children of our friends, the Kramers, they would jump onto and between the rocks, trying not to fall off and disturb the carefully arranged small stones beneath. They would be hooting with laughter (hopefully not disturbing too much the people on silent retreat!). Some years later, our daughter was complaining during one meal-time that we never used to take them to France on holiday, 'Like EVERYONE else.' I pointed out that we took them to Belgium. 'Yeah,' said our eldest, derisively, 'to a monastery!'

During the time of Lockdown I made regular visits to some old and faithful sacred spaces and to one or two newly discovered ones as well. My early morning walk often takes me through the woods on the way up to Kent University and they are filled in April with bluebells. It's one of the first places that Yim Soon and I took our first child Kieran in 1995 when he was about ten weeks old. When I'm in those woods at that time of year I can always picture carrying him in a baby sling through the bluebells. Another sacred space is the area outside my shed at the bottom of the garden, and when it's warm enough I sit there after the morning walk with a cup of tea, listening to the birds and watching the sun rise over the trees. I sit there as well in the late afternoon, with another cup of tea, and listen to the birds again and, depending on the time of year, maybe watch the sun start to go down.

I did a lot of cycling in those days, and there is one particular route that I never tired of. It takes me out of Canterbury via Clowes Wood and then on a long, straight stretch through Thornden Wood and West Blean Wood, and near the end of which is a bench where I always stop. It's in memory of a lovely young woman called Alison who died in 1997. I knew her a little bit, also her mother Bried, who must still be going there regularly, since the flowerpots around the bench are always well tended. I have a little sit on the bench and say a little prayer about anything that might be troubling me. I might then do an extra section through East Blean Wood but either way, I end up eventually in Herne Bay.

For a few weeks, when it was almost the only place open, I would go to the petrol station on the main street and get a latte from the machine, which I would then drink next to the pier, near the spot where I met Sam McCallum, the Coventry City left-back. When Makcaris Coffee Parlour opened up again at the Central Bandstand I started going there for my latte, plus a delicious home-made chocolate flapjack; and I would have a little bit of banter with the friendly Romanian man who always served me.

Following my sit by the sea, it's back along the coast to Whitstable, with a quick stop when I reach the Hotel Continental to take in the view. I've drunk a lot of cups of tea there (occasionally something a little stronger), while sitting looking out over the sea towards the Isle of Sheppey, and, on a clear day, all the way to Southend on the other side of the Thames Estuary. The return to Canterbury is via the Crab and Winkle Line which was the route for many years of the final day of the annual L'Arche Kent pilgrimage, so there are loads of special memories both of that and of other walks, runs and cycles.

Another sacred space for me became the Facebook Livestream of Taizé Evening Prayer, which went out daily for about three months. Taizé is an inter-denominational monastic community in the South of France which uses in its three-time daily prayer short songs, or chants, which are in different languages, in four parts, and sung over and over. It's a very accessible, inclusive and uplifting way to pray. Also, during the time of social isolation, it was important for me to feel in connection with people from all over the world. I went there faithfully every evening at 7.30, and it even got me out of the washing-up sometimes ('Sorry, got to go to Taizé now'). Taizé is an incredibly special place for me. I've been there several times over the years, and Yim Soon and I have even been there with the children (so it's not true that we never took them to France!). And actually, one of the other times that we went was when Yim Soon was five months pregnant with Kieran, so he's been there twice: as well as his three trips to Belgium!

Thank God for sacred spaces. I'll be sure to keep returning to them …

59. NEW TECHNOLOGY

We thought we were getting good at Zoom at the Irish Chaplaincy: just click on the link and you're in. Simple!? So I was completely thrown when we were suddenly being asked for passwords for the Monday 11 a.m. meeting that I'd set up the week before, when there didn't seem to be any mention of passwords. And as if there isn't enough stress, and passwords, in our life already! There was a frantic flurry of emails and phone calls and in the end I sent a new invitation, and confirmed what the password was, and one by one the faces appeared on the screen, to my huge relief. And there was always a palpable sense of joy, during the time of Lockdown, when we saw each other and had the chance to connect.

Having survived the little password drama, I thought I would finally attempt to set up a YouTube live stream, for what I hoped might be the broadcasting of mini-concerts into care homes, and other things. I'd watched a couple of YouTube videos about it and thought, 'Come on, you can do it!' I successfully downloaded the required OBS (Open Broadcaster Software), as recommended in one of the videos, and found and entered the relevant password (honestly, they will be the death of me!), and was encouraged when my face appeared on the screen and I could, or so I believed, start broadcasting. But I couldn't for the life of me connect it up properly with my YouTube channel. I toiled and stressed through lunch-time and had to admit defeat in the end as I had a 2 p.m. Zoom: for which I'd made sure I'd sent the password! The problem was, because of my face now being on the OBS screen, even when I thought I'd closed it, it wasn't appearing on the Zoom screen! More stress! Thankfully my daughter was at home at the time and she sorted out the issue. Another panic over … until the next one.

Whenever these little technological trials take place, I think of an incident on a bus in Estonia in January 2013. Yim Soon and I had been invited to the country by some lovely Estonian women at L'Arche, and I'd been instructed to call Leeni when we got on a bus from Tallinn airport to say what time we'd arrive in their city, Tartu, where they would meet us. My phone was a cast-off from one of the children and it was one of those where the keypad slid out. I thought it was pretty cool! Problem was, I couldn't find the '+' symbol, in order to make an international call. I asked a young man on the bus, 'Do you speak English?' 'Of course!' (fluently). 'Can you help me with my phone?'. He found the '+' and I called Leeni and it was all okay, and then I said to him, 'I'm not very good with new technology.' He looked at my slide-out phone. 'This is not new technology,' he said, 'this is history!' We ended up for the remaining couple of hours of the journey talking and sharing our stories and Yim Soon, meanwhile, was chatting away happily with a young woman on the other side of the bus. The man confided to me that Estonians didn't normally speak to strangers on buses, but that he had really enjoyed it. I had too.

That episode revealed to me a deeper truth which seems especially relevant at times of crisis. When we lose our usual self-reliance and have to ask for help then people open up to one another and the most incredible things start to happen.

By the way, I gave up in the end with the YouTube Live Stream. A man can only take so much stress! I recorded instead a couple of mini-concerts via zoom which I then shared with interested parties. No passwords were needed …

60. KEEPING CONNECTED

There were a couple of revealing pieces in the press in relation to the first lockdown. The *Observer* published the results of a survey that showed that just 20 per cent of the British public wanted an early easing of the lockdown. And an article in the *Times* the following day had the headline: 'Six weeks in and the house is spotless, but you've got serious Zoom fatigue.'

I was still liking Zoom, although I tried to limit it to two per working day, plus an occasional 'social' zoom in the evening. One such social was a 'beer zoom' I'd planned to have on a Friday with a good friend and I had a couple of cans chilling in the fridge in preparation, and even had a picture of a pub ready as a zoom virtual background! In the end, my friend had to cancel, declaring himself 'Zoom dead'; and anyway, I'd come down to the kitchen on the Friday morning to discover my cans by the sink, empty, together with a couple of similarly empty bottles. Our youngest had been doing another virtual session with his mates the night before. He had clearly not tired yet of Zoom catch-ups and quizzes and beers with a variety of groups.

I very much enjoyed speaking to my mum via Skype, and it was touching to see the mutual excitement when I passed the laptop on to the two of her grandchildren who were at home during the lockdown and for them to exchange a few words. The Irish Chaplaincy Seniors' Project began a trial of a new project which came to be called 'Keeping Connected', by which we hoped to supply some of those elderly, isolated Irish that we support with electronic Tablets. Besides giving the opportunity for face-to-face conversation, they would have various things programmed in; like Masses from Ireland, with just a swipe or a touch of the screen needed.

LOOKING AHEAD WITH HOPE

There was another first for me a few weeks into that first lockdown: my first Zoom meeting in French. This truly was a time for trying new things. It was fun! It was the team who organises the annual L'Arche retreat in the French Alps, cancelled like everything else in the COVID year. One of the participants at the meeting, Alienor, was sitting out in her garden in the South of France! Another, Odile, told of how two of the learning-disabled women in the L'Arche house where she helps had died of COVID-19 but that nobody had been able to see the bodies or attend any kind of funeral service. 'It's like they just disappeared,' she remarked, sadly. I explained how moved I'd been to be part of a Zoom remembrance service, with almost forty others, for my friend Pam.

In relation to the *Observer* poll, I was very much part of the 80 per cent who were reluctant to see a quick easing of lockdown. When I'd mentioned that to a priest in London he'd replied, 'I agree. Some of us have a great deal to be thankful for and while others are having a rough time it is unseemly to be bemoaning one's lot in between bread-making, Zoom parties and the like. It's given me time to think as well without having to struggle for the time. So I'm with the 80 per cent too.' I know as he does that this period was not kind to everyone. Calls to domestic abuse helplines shot up; a lot of people were losing their jobs; and many of the elderly Irish we support were feeling lonely and isolated even before the coronavirus came along.

But I also relished the time to think and to live life a little more simply and a little more slowly; and to be able to take the time to see and hear and smell and touch the things of such incredible beauty in our garden and elsewhere. I was grateful for having two of our children at home with us for almost six months, so too for my 'virtual' connections, and with those people, known or unknown, who I bumped into when out on my daily exercise. How nice that we were not all in such a hurry during those days.

And, like the 80 per cent in the survey, I was in no great hurry to return to 'normal'.

61. LESSONS FROM LOCKDOWN

When the initial lockdown first began I'd been quite unnerved by the closed shops and the empty streets. And I had watched in dismay as the cafés had closed one by one, wondering how on earth I was going to work at home every day, and with a household that had doubled in size. I got used to it very quickly: my 'smaller' world; the lovely presence of two of our children, and with our eldest, Kieran, calling us most weeks for a family catch up. It was a slower, simpler day to day existence. I relished the daily bike rides to the sea and I really got used to having the seafront all to myself, to the point that I resented the returning crowds! I knew I shouldn't be selfish (it's their seaside as well, I suppose!), but I knew as well that I'd need to be gentle with myself as the world began returning to some form of 'normality'.

Routines had to change during the lockdown, and I was struck by how much I hadn't missed. When the garden centres re-opened, Yim Soon and I climbed into the car one Sunday morning to join the queues at our nearest Nursery and I realised that it was the first time in weeks that I'd driven anywhere. I really hadn't missed it. I enjoyed working in London, one of the most interesting and vibrant and green cities in the world, but I hadn't missed the daily commute: and those early morning hours are my most creative and productive of the day. I certainly didn't miss roads filled with traffic. I usually like to travel and a few special trips had been cancelled but found that I didn't really miss that. And I was interested to hear another priest in London tell me that he is normally glued to televised football or GAA sports, or any kind of sport, but hadn't missed it, and I replied, 'Neither have I; it's as if all of that belongs to a different world.'

On my way back from the sea one day I bumped into Tony, an old friend from football and a big Liverpool fan. I asked him what he thought should be done about the reminder of the Premier League season: with his team needing just two wins from nine remaining games to secure their first league title in thirty years. 'Do you know what, Ed,' he replied, 'this might sound strange, but I really don't care! I've met a new woman, I'm in love, and I'm getting paid to do nothing! These have been the best two months of my life.' Wow! This really had been a time to re-evaluate our priorities.

What did *I* learn from that time? I'm not sure it was learning, rather coming to a deeper appreciation of some of those things which bring joy and meaning to my life. I had a lovely little booklet that had been given to people at a St Brigid's event at the Irish Embassy, and I made this my 'Gratitude Diary' during the period of the first lockdown. Here are some of the entries:

Birds singing, bees buzzing, morning tea and prayer outside the shed, gorgeous red sky and frost at 6 a.m., trees coming into bloom, nice chat with Miran, long bike ride with Sean, star-filled sky, Taizé Evening prayer, Zoom with a friend, connecting with the team at the Irish Chaplaincy, tulips, two cups of tea and Miran and Sean's chocolate cake eaten outside the shed at the end of a glorious sunny afternoon, walk in the woods with Yim Soon, Skype with mum, blue skies, good day's work, sound of rainfall, good food, bluebells, garden looking lovely. One entry concluded with the line, 'Another good, simple day'.

There was one entry which made me smile: 'reconciliation with Yim Soon after getting annoyed with her at the meal'! I don't even remember now what that was about but am thankful that it got sorted out somehow! We were lucky; a lot of relationships were coming under a lot of strain at that time.

The lockdown would come to an end and the coronavirus would presumably, at some point, be fully contained, and I suspected that we'd return to most of our pre-virus practices. And I expected that I would be happy, in most respects, to do so: travelling to interesting places, for work or on holiday; meeting people in the flesh; going to the gym; singing with my choir; even sharing the seaside with loads of other people: at least the cafés would be open again.

But I hoped that I would continue to take a bit of time each day to sit, weather permitting, at the bottom of the garden with a nice cup of tea, listening to the birds; to connect with and cherish my family and friends; to write; to be open to whatever encounter or experience each day would bring. I wanted to carry on being content with simple pleasures; and I hoped I'd never again take for granted going into a shop and finding a loaf of bread on the shelf.

Above all, I hoped I would be grateful for each and every day, and for whatever is given.

P.S. When Liverpool finally got over the line to win the league, Tony was over the moon. He really did care!

62. HOW TO BE HAPPY FOREVER

There are varying suggestions for attaining eternal happiness, depending, amongst many other things, on whether you read an English proverb or a Chinese one.

According to the English proverb: 'If you want to be happy for a year, plant a garden; If you want to be happy for life, plant a tree.'

I'm very lucky to have a garden, and I can say that it has been a place of pleasure, prayer, play, produce and performance; rest, rejuvenation and recreation; health, healing, hospitality, harvest, and good honest hard graft: year after year and in all seasons. It was a particular place of solace during the coronavirus pandemic, and I had a bit more time than usual to simply enjoy the sacred space. I remarked to my son one day, 'I'm sure the birds have been singing more loudly during the lockdown.' He replied, 'It's just that you'd usually be working in an office in London and wouldn't be able to hear them or wouldn't be listening to them!' Maybe that's true; but I was still convinced that they were singing more loudly. It was actually proven that the birds were singing *less* loudly during lockdown, due to the absence of competing noises like traffic! I even became a little more aware of the many different tunes of the song thrush. I'm ashamed to say that I would have assumed that each species of bird sang the same song all the time. But no, these guys can really mix it up and have a party.

I love during the summer being able to sit out in the garden in the early morning and listen to those birds, and to look at the flowers and to smell the fragrant roses and shrubs, so carefully shaped over many years. And then I like to sit out again in the late afternoon or early evening and to listen to those birds again and to rejoice in the beauty and the peace, and to give thanks for another day.

Turning to the Chinese proverb about happiness, we are told that: 'If you want happiness for an hour, take a nap. If you want happiness for a day, go fishing. If you want happiness for a month, get married. If you want happiness for a year, inherit a fortune. If you want happiness for a lifetime, help someone else.'

We were blessed at the Irish Chaplaincy with many new volunteers at the start of the lockdown, and I was touched to read what one of them, Kristjana, had written, following her contact with Phyllis:

'When I got involved in shopping and delivering for the elderly with the Irish Chaplaincy, I was not expecting it to be such a gratifying and eye-opening experience. Though most encounters today are timid and reserved, my first with Phyllis was not. Phyllis is a wonderfully bright, inquisitive, chipper, straight-talking lady. She has shared with me the things that distress her, snippets of her life and her general day-to-day happenings. It has been a pleasure sharing these with her, talking about the very mundane to the very serious. She thanks me numerous times each time I deliver the shop. But I don't think she realises how grateful I am for her and the experiences. The opportunity to commit some time and to help my community in this way has been a humbling and lovely experience.'

I think those English and Chinese proverbs may be more connected than seems apparent at a first reading. When we tend a garden we are giving pleasure to others as well as to ourselves, and bringing forth something of beauty will surely give benefits far beyond our own life, and to people we'll never meet. As said earlier, Dostoevsky made the interesting claim that beauty will save the world. In the case of planting a tree it is all the more striking that it will bring benefits to future generations long after the planter has departed from the earth.

And one further connection: the Chinese character for 'rest' is composed of the character for 'person' next to that for 'tree', which seems rather fitting.

Finding happiness is not a straightforward business, and we must beware of chasing it too keenly, for as the Hasidic proverb warns us: 'While we pursue happiness, we flee from contentment'. But if we truly desire to be happy forever, having some beautiful spaces to enjoy certainly helps. In writing that, I'm well aware that many people don't have such spaces. And let us spare a particular thought for prisoners, whose cells during the summer are like ovens, and who, during lockdown, were confined to them for up to 23.5 hours a day. Maybe, as the Chinese would have it, we just need to help someone: or to allow ourselves to be helped; because, ultimately, we're all interconnected, and one is not possible without the other. It's as simple, or as difficult, as that.

63. KEEPING ON KEEPING ON

At the start of another day of lockdown I was reminded of a remark made to me by an American man called John who I met while walking on the Camino in Spain.

I'd woken up early, as I usually did in those days, and thought, without a huge amount of enthusiasm, 'Oh, another day; do I really have to!' It had been a good week up until that point, and a couple of important meetings and presentations which had required a lot of preparation and energy had gone well. But I was feeling a little drained and flat in the aftermath and wondering how I was going to find some new motivation for a day in which there were no especially 'big' things happening: like a lot of days really during the lockdown! I managed, somehow, to remove myself from the comfort of the bed and to get out for my morning walk. And I tried to tell myself how lucky I was to be able to do such a thing, when some of those prisoners supported by the Irish Chaplaincy were being allowed out of their cell for just thirty minutes a day, and were faced with an unenviable choice: to have a shower, to join a long queue for the phone (assuming they had the means to make a call), or to go into the exercise yard, where there may not be too much social distancing.

I followed exactly the same route I had for the previous fortnight or so, which was through the bluebell wood on the way up to the Kent University campus. I didn't want to miss a single day of the bluebells, although they were starting to fade so I could maybe begin walking somewhere else! Mix it up a bit! There's a wonderfully fragrant yellow azalea which had just come into bloom in the cemetery near us so that became a favourite place to go in subsequent weeks.

My life in lockdown become a bit monastic, and there was a lot I liked about that. There was quite a nice, simple balance of work, prayer, meals, reading, and recreation: much of that in the form of walking or cycling. I was a bit more tuned in than usual to the subtle but magical changes in the natural world: the colours and the smells, the times of the day when the birds sing more loudly, the wonderful sight in the sky one night of a crescent moon underneath a brightly shining Venus.

But any routine can also become a bit monotonous, and even my taking part every day without fail in the Facebook Live-stream of Evening prayer from Taizé was not quite as 'uplifting' as it had been in the first week or two. And I was clearly not the only one who was feeling like that. In the beginning there were close to 4,000 people tuning in. After a few weeks the viewing figures were down to 2,000! What were those vanished 2,000 doing instead, I wondered?

Most days I was fairly content with this simple life but there were some days when I thought, 'Oh, I just want to get in the car or on a train or on a plane and, well, just go somewhere… anywhere.' It's often tempting to want to 'get away', in the belief that we'll somehow be more content or more stimulated or more this or more that if only we were in a different place. I was struck by Gerry's piece in the Irish Chaplaincy Easter newsletter, 'A Time to be Still', where he mentioned that in the 1650s the French philosopher and mathematician Blaise Pascal made a perceptive comment about the human condition. 'The sole cause of a person's unhappiness,' he said, 'is that they cannot stay quietly in their room.' There is even a word and a phrase in the monastic tradition to describe this restlessness: because imagine being in an actual monastery and following exactly the same routine every day, every week for, say, fifty years! It's called 'acedia' (from the Greek '*akedia*', meaning indifference), or the 'noonday demon', and it's a kind of listlessness, when the simplest of acts can take a huge effort. It's when I can't quite find the motivation or the enthusiasm to do anything, and the temptation is to want to escape from the mundane, the humdrum, the routine. Although I know deep down that if I can't be content here and now, I'll never be content in some other place with some other people doing some other thing.

It was when I was feeling rather out of sorts and out of energy one morning that I met John, a fellow pilgrim. Yes, the 'noonday demon' can strike anywhere, even on the magical, mystical Camino to Santiago. We got chatting and John, who'd grown up in Tennessee, told me about how he'd just taken early retirement at the age of fifty from a highly stressful career in hotel hospitality in California. I asked if he had any hopes or dreams for his fiftieth birthday year, and beyond. 'Weeelll,' he replied in his slow, Southern drawl, 'Aaaahh just wanna keep ooon keeping oooon!'

My encounter with John helped lift me out of that particular little trough, and I often think of his words. And may we all, whatever our circumstances, find somehow the strength to keep on keeping on.

64. KEEPING CONNECTED (PART II)

'It's the nicest thing anyone has done for me. I felt so lonely during lockdown. Now I feel so connected.'

So said Ann, who is supported by the Irish Chaplaincy Seniors' Project and who was one of the first recipients of a pre-programmed Tablet, via our 'Keeping Connected' project. Rory, one of the Seniors team, explained: 'Ann really loved it. I called over to her yesterday to see if she was getting on okay with it. She was there listening to LMFM, her favourite (Drogheda-based) radio station. She was thrilled with it.' Ann went on to say, 'With this Tablet, I've been able to see my nephew, my friends in London and even my friends in Ireland. I love listening to the Irish radio and getting Mass. I can't thank you enough.'

Paul and I had discussed at the start of lockdown how we might be able to use technology to keep people better connected but we were both a little unsure about how or even whether it would work to provide people with electronic devices. Then one of our wonderful volunteers Joe came up with a cunning plan involving Tablets, dongles and Giffgaff-activated SIM cards! We decided to trial it with a few people and Declan ordered a first batch of Tablets and programmed them so that things could be easily accessed by pressing an icon on the screen or swiping. And there's an option for him to give remote help to the holder of the Tablet. He also made some easy to follow instructions.

The next question was how to deliver the Tablets. Another

of our wonderful volunteers, Martina, had returned in March 2020 from cycling round the world for two years with her husband. She was ready to cycle some more, and pedalled around London making the initial deliveries. The first recipient was eighty-nine-year-old Mamie who has been supported by the Chaplaincy for many years. 'I'm so excited to try this out,' said Mamie when the Tablet came out of the box. 'I can now speak to you all face to face at the Chaplaincy and plan to speak to my sister (who lives in Galway) for her 100th birthday.'

I was touched to see the first pictures of 'Keeping Connected' in action: Ann holding up her Tablet, and Mamie sitting watching Pentecost Mass from her local parish in Archway. She said afterwards that she was going to use the Tablet to call Fr Ugo, her parish priest. And another of her first actions with the new device was to join Facebook. Ann added that she was thrilled with the Tablet and said it was the best gift she'd ever had and couldn't believe she'd got it! She had never used a computer or Tablet before, but said she was getting on with it well.

I was so pleased that people like Ann and Mamie were seeing the possibilities that this technology can offer. I hoped we'd be able to find the funds to supply many more people with Tablets, and I was confident that our 'Keeping Connected' project would last well beyond the lockdown.

65. COMING OUT OF LOCKDOWN

I wasn't sure which felt more strange: going into lockdown or coming out of it.

A lot of things had apparently returned to 'normal' after the first lockdown but it didn't take long to realise that they were not very 'normal' at all and neither would they be for some time to come, if ever. A case in point was places of worship. I was initially excited to hear that Canterbury Cathedral had reopened to visitors, albeit at the slightly odd hours of 4.30 p.m. – 8 p.m.; and I decided to attend Evensong in the first week that it was up and running again. On the way there I called into St Thomas's, my local church, and was pleased to bump into Fr Anthony. We had a long chat and were both agreed that these were 'interesting times'! I popped inside for a little pray and was a little disconcerted by the tape preventing access to every other pew; also by the fact that as soon as I left, somebody came to disinfect where I'd been sitting. It's completely understandable and necessary but it just felt a bit peculiar and, for me at any rate, not terribly conducive to a prayerful atmosphere.

After an exiting handwash at the church, I walked the short distance to the Cathedral (passing on the way a couple wearing what looked like gas masks!) and once inside that grand building my hands were disinfected once more and I had my name and number taken, in case I needed to be tracked and traced. Only then was I allowed to pass on through another lot of barriers and one-way systems. Evensong was now being held in the vast nave, and I was one of six members of the congregation, together with the four celebrants and the verger. That's the person who leads the celebrants to their positions whilst holding a big rod, or 'virge'. She looked very unsure of where she was supposed to be leading them. These 'new normals' were taking some getting used to for all of us! We were all miles from one another, let alone two metres, and needless to say there were none of the usual choir boys with their angelic voices. I was truly grateful that these places of worship had opened their doors again and for all the planning and hard work that had made it possible, but there was something very clinical and odd about the whole thing. Religion, for me, is about bringing people together, not keeping them far apart!

A couple of days later, I was having a (socially-distanced!) cup of tea with a friend, a dyed in the wool Catholic like me. She told me how in recent months she had particularly felt the presence of God on her daily walks through the woods, and that she was in no hurry to return to Mass in the physical building. Like many, she had been attending, and enjoying, Mass regularly on-line.

As I mentioned to Fr Anthony, it would be interesting to see how many people would ever go back to attending a service in the physical church building now that they were so used to watching from the comfort of their own home. St Thomas's had a decent webcam installed and the plan was to continue the live-streaming of Masses in the longer-term and I think that is sensible. The Irish Chaplaincy's 'Keeping Connected' campaign has shown the huge potential of supplying elderly people with electronic devices, and making them relatively straightforward to use, and with which they can access Mass or a favourite radio station, besides having face to face conversations, and with people anywhere in the world. John, the Galwayman who I spoke to every week was delighted with his Tablet, and proudly told me how he'd listened to Galway

Bay FM, had looked at the *Tuam Herald* on-line and had spoken, via Duo, with his friend Pat, one of our volunteers. He had said to Martina, who had delivered the Tablet and helped him get started on it, 'This has been a great day.'

Pandemics through the ages have often led to significant, and positive, social change. The cholera epidemic in London in the nineteenth century led to government investment in clean drinking water and proper sanitation. The Spanish Flu of 1918/19 highlighted (as did COVID-19) the inequality between social classes and led to a better understanding, in some countries at least, of the importance of universal healthcare and low-income housing.

It remained to be seen what kind of long-term social change would result from the coronavirus, but significant change there would be and I hoped that much of that change might be positive. If one of the consequences was that some people at least were enabled to be more connected, with each other, with their faith and their culture, and with the world around them, albeit 'virtually', then surely that had to be a good thing.

And one final thought: it seemed that arrows would be part of our lives for some time to come, whether telling us how to go into and out of a restaurant or just which way to walk down a shopping street, and I was tickled to see that some of them were yellow. The Camino in Spain shows pilgrims the way to Santiago by lots of clearly and carefully placed … yellow arrows! Maybe that was a good omen.

66. ZOOM RETREAT

I've always enjoyed being on retreat and I've always enjoyed helping to lead retreats, and the Irish Chaplaincy Summer Retreat via Zoom conference was no disappointment.

In the middle of the week it was remarked on in our retreat team check-in that a real sense of community had been established amongst the participants. And I'd been struck by the comment of Catherine in that morning's session how even people not on the retreat were being touched by what was happening. She had shared with friends the recordings of each day's reflection and noted how 'Ripples were spreading outwards'.

Even if there was a set format to each morning's session, every day was slightly different, so too the composition of the group, as we'd made it clear from the outset that people could attend as many or as few of the sessions as they could, and were free to fit the sessions into their 'normal' daily life. Although, who knew what normal was anymore! I would play a little bit of instrumental music on the guitar as people arrived on screen, with my friend Jenny playing the flute one day, then once all were assembled I'd read out any little messages from participants regarding their experience of the previous day, and share any photos that had been sent. One very special picture was of Ann on a bench at the coast in South Wales overlooking the sea. And it turned out that Ann lived two roads away from my sister in Coventry, and knew as well the street where my dad had lived in digs in the 50s. Ann's bench had been put there in memory of her parents and at the spot where she and her Welsh mother and Irish father would sit and rest and watch the sea and the Irish ferry coming into Swansea docks. I had mentioned in my reflection on the first day, in the context of sacred spaces, a bench in my garden where I had often sat in the first weeks of the lockdown, and this bench had featured on the retreat poster. I'd then sing a little meditative song and we would be together in silence for four minutes and what a rich silence that was. It was followed by a reflection from a different member of the team, and the themes included: 'Go into the mountains', 'He touched me', 'Life to the full: finding your treasure', and 'Looking ahead with hope'.

There would be a final song, and a blessing from a different person each day. And the retreat concluded with a blessing and a message of hope from Cardinal Vincent Nichols, and with each person saying what they were thankful for about the week. Some of the comments were:

'I found this "remote" retreat very helpful and a great source of spiritual nurture.'

'A real blessing to have this time of being quiet, and to be part of this new little community.'

'Very uplifting.'

'Thank you for reminding us to take things more relaxed and notice things we wouldn't otherwise see.'

I know how important music is on retreat, and at events and in life generally, and had the privilege of sharing some of my own favourites. This included on the first day a song of my own that I'd written when I'd been on retreat the year before in North Wales. On the Tuesday I'd chosen the well-known hymn 'I watch the Sunrise' and explained that it had been written by John Glynn, when convalescing, in the very house of the Mercy sisters at Clacton-on-Sea where Moira and Kathleen live now and where we've spent a couple of Irish Chaplaincy Away Days. Following the session I received a message from one of the group, Clodagh, to say: 'That song was played at my mum's funeral; she was the very epitome of sunshine to everyone she met; and it is coming up to her first year anniversary. I think she was sending me a lovely sign through you. Thank you.' That showed me again how we touch one another, and create little ripples, in ways we may never even know.

It was a privilege and a pleasure for us as a team to organise and to participate in the week, and we were all agreed that there would be more Irish Chaplaincy Zoom retreats to come.

Incidentally, Kathleen is one of the nuns I've danced with since being at the Chaplaincy. At the end of Mass on one of our Clacton Away Days we waltzed out of the convent chapel together, and how lovely and joyful that was.

67. PRAYING TWICE

It was Saint Augustine who said that to sing was to pray twice. At a time when singing was not allowed in churches it was wonderful to be at the monastery and to be able to sing during the chapel services.

It was wonderful in general to be back at the monastery, a place I've made regular visits to for almost thirty years. It only reopened to guests in August 2020, after closing its doors in March due to the coronavirus, and I was one of the first on the list. I couldn't wait! In a year when various trips were cancelled, it was the first time in six months that I'd slept in a different bed. I'd been saying to participants at the start of the Chaplaincy retreat that sometimes it's good to go to another place, a place apart, for it is only then, perhaps, that we have the opportunity to see things a bit differently or to really notice things that we may not normally notice. The first thing I noticed on arrival at the monastery was how tired I was, even after being off work for a week. That week had been a 'staycation' and it had been very nice, but I just needed to spend a bit of time on my own, and, yes, to be in a different place.

I slept long and deep on the first night and after waking up I looked out of the window at the trees and the rising sun and went for a first stroll in the woods, then to the chapel for what would be my first service of the day, the 7 a.m. 'Lauds'. The monks had already prayed 'Vigils' at 5 a.m. but I was never going to be joining them for that. I was on holiday after all! There's something very calming and ordering and centring about the monastic liturgy. Various psalms are sung in plainchant, with one side of the chapel singing one verse and the other side singing the next, so that there is a constant give and take, an ebb and flow. Breakfast follows, eaten in silence, and with social distancing observed in the refectory! The monastery is a place for me of sacred rituals and one such is the second cup of tea. One of the monks goes around the tables mid-way through breakfast with a tray, onto which we place our empty mugs. He pours from the large tea pot at the side, and goes around again with the tray from which we pick up our now full mug of steaming hot tea. That something so simple as receiving a second cup of tea in the morning can produce in me such delight indicates how special the place is.

It's only just gone 8 a.m. when breakfast is finished. There is a whole day ahead. That day will be punctuated by more services and by more meals. There is the short mid-day office, 'Sext', followed by lunch, the main meal of the day. And there is 'Vespers' in the evening. The exact order and timings of the services varies according to the monastery but here, as in all monasteries, the final liturgy of the day is followed by the 'great silence', a time when a particular hush descends until the following morning.

I sink into that silence, and I luxuriate in the stillness and in the ancient, wholesome and healing monastic rhythms. I go for long walks in the surrounding countryside, and for short, slow meanders in the monastery grounds. I read a bit, write a bit, rest a bit. I sit out in the garden in the late afternoon sun with a cup of tea; and then walk barefoot in the orchard in grass that's still long and lush and green in spite of the recent heatwave.

I give thanks for this place of peace, of rest and rejuvenation, of simple pleasures. And I rejoice that I'm able to sing and therefore, according to St Augustine, to pray twice.

68. THE GIFT THAT KEEPS ON GIVING

I was picking up my bike from the repair shop and there came to mind something that Breda had said in the summer retreat, when speaking of her work with people in prison: 'If you can be kind, be kind.'

I'd been folding up my commuter bike to store it in the shed, as it seemed I wouldn't be needing it again for some time, and something snapped so that the handlebars kept falling down! It seemed at first that I'd need to buy a new bike, and then I thought, 'No, maybe Chris can do something with it; it's worth a try at any rate.' Chris runs the bike shop in Canterbury that I've been going to for many years. I bought bikes there for all three of my children and one for myself, and I've always gone there for repairs. And when doing a repair, they had often done a little extra something for free.

The shop has been through a few incarnations over the years: 'Tibbs Cycles', 'Canterbury Cycle Centre', 'Canterbury Cycle Lab'. Then with the onset of COVID, Chris decided to stop selling bikes, which he told me wasn't making any money, and to concentrate on repairs: which presumably does make money! The shop has duly been reborn as 'Bicycle Repairs - Canterbury', and like many things these days (going to the gym; even attending Mass in some places!) you can't just turn up; you have to book on-line.

I booked my slot and took my 'Dahon' into Chris and he said they might be able to fix it. And fix it they did, just by gluing together a plastic thing that had snapped and reinserting it in the correct place. I was really relieved I wouldn't have the expense and the hassle of getting a replacement bike and asked Chris how much I owed him. 'That's alright,' he said, 'it was only a small job.' I was so happy to be on the receiving end of that little act of kindness, and almost danced out of the shop. And I sort of wondered how I could be kind, in turn, to somebody that day. For kindness really does beget kindness.

As well as Breda's comment, I recalled an interesting recent incident when we were having a new freezer delivered. I got chatting to the two young guys who carried it in, and one of them explained to me, rather apologetically, that they couldn't take the packaging away. 'Oh, not to worry,' I said, 'I wasn't expecting that.' His colleagues spotted my Ovation guitar that happened to be sitting in the corner of the room. 'That's a beautiful guitar,' he remarked. I said he was welcome to have a go on it, and ended up telling the story of how a complete stranger had given it to me twenty-five years before and how I'd always felt fairly free about sharing it, and how it had served me and others well. 'The gift that keeps on giving,' he said. And then the first guy said, 'We're going to take the packaging away for you; it's nice when people appreciate us.' I was so touched.

On the same day that I was picking up my bike from the shop I listened to a phone message Fiona had sent me from a man in prison who said, 'I can't ever thank you all enough for what you've done for me throughout my sentence.' He's been in prison for most of his life and has decided now that he wants our help to get out and stay out; including referral to drug rehab. As with many people coming out of prison, he has a mountain to climb but the fact that he is asking for help is a hopeful sign. And we'll just never know where an act of kindness may lead.

69. LOOKING AHEAD WITH HOPE

In the Spring of 2021, the coronavirus continued to have a huge impact on our lives, and people and countries around the world were facing an uncertain future. There had been some semblance of a return to 'normality' following a third lockdown. Shops, cafés, and pubs were gradually re-opening; places of worship were admitting limited numbers, as long as certain measures were in place; and my gym finally began to let some people in to use machines carefully screened off from one another. Many people, though, were cautious about returning and it was a similar story with the churches. And whilst COVID-19 infection and death rates had dropped, for the time being at least, in the UK, elsewhere in the world they were still rising. New strains of the virus were causing new problems, vaccination rates were unequal across the globe, and several countries had reimposed lockdowns.

Global economies would surely take decades to recover from the pandemic, and people's habits around work, leisure, public worship, travel etc may never again be exactly what they were pre-COVID-19. I suspected that we'd have to re-think, in particular, how (or even whether) we use physical buildings when so much now could be done on-line. How and where would we choose to work, shop, spend our leisure time, attend religious services? What would become of our town and city centres with the inevitable closure of yet more shops and businesses?

And what could be said about hope at such a time? I'd been

struck by a comment of the Dominican Timothy Radcliffe in an article called 'Living Well in Lockdown':

'So when our habitual calendars are shredded and we have no idea when this pestilence will pass, the secret is to live our days as shaped by hope.'

Radcliffe went on in his article to quote the Baptist theologian, Ian Stackhouse:

'It seems to me that the battle for civilisation will pivot on the outrageously simple challenge of living a day well.'

Could it be that one of the opportunities offered by this crisis was the chance to re-evaluate how we live our lives, and how we spend our days? The Irish Chaplaincy exists in part to bring hope to some of those people who may be living lives of quiet despair, and during the pandemic we continued to help some in especially tough circumstances with that universal challenge of living a day well. We provided prisoners with in-cell resources like books, CDs, puzzles, and mindful-colouring at a time when some were confined to their cells for up to 23.5 hours per day and with no family visits, activities, education or work. I'd been especially touched by the response of a woman in HMP Bronzefield, who had been helped in this way:

'The colouring book is so lovely, means so much, made me cry. I love felt tip pens also, really helps me with mental health side.'

For some of the elderly Irish supported, the pre-programmed Tablets supplied as part of our 'Keeping connected' campaign were a lifeline. John told me each week when I spoke to him on the phone how he loved using his Tablet for listening to Galway Bay FM in the evening and speaking face to face with his friend Pat. As I wrote earlier, he'd remarked to Martina after she'd cycled over to Hammersmith and set him up with his Tablet, 'This has been a great day.'

I'm privileged to find myself part of an organisation which chimes so much with my own values and background. I'm thankful for the opportunity to work with and to meet such a host of interesting and inspiring people. I delight in the remarkable connections which bind us together in our common humanity; and I find that the words of the French Jesuit Jean-Pierre de Caussade from his book *The Sacrament of the Present Moment* written about 300 years ago still hold true:

'The more a soul loves, the more it longs, the more it hopes, the more it finds.'

I will try to have an open heart, so that I might receive with gratitude what is given in each moment, in each day, and in each encounter. And whatever an uncertain future may hold, I will continue to look ahead with hope.

ACKNOWLEDGEMENTS

Special thanks go to those who read part or all of an early manuscript. To Mary, who first planted the seed of an idea for a book and for frequent kind words and inspiration, besides the sage advice to lose some of the brackets! To Kieran for his helpful and perceptive comments and for telling me to lose some of the commas! To Adrian for suggestions about where exactly the book should begin. To John for his encouragement, and for offering to publicise a book long before one even existed. To Chris for recommending that I approach DLT. And to Helen and Will and all at DLT, and in particular to David, for making it happen.

Thanks as well to Paul for suggesting the main title, and to the Averbecks for bringing me back to that after I'd strayed.

Thanks to all at the Irish Chaplaincy, without whom none of this would have happened; and thanks to my dear family and friends.

PERMISSIONS

'The Magi' is used with permission of the UK Jesuits.

The 'Oscar Romero Prayer' is used with permission of the Romero Trust.